D0379319

# The Cunning Linguist

## Also by Richard Lederer

Anguished English
The Biggest Book of Animal Riddles (with James Ertner)
The Bride of Anguished English
The Circus of Words
Crazy English
Dictionary of Americanisms (with John Russell Bartlett)
Fractured English
Get Thee to a Punnery
Have a Punny Christmas
Literary Trivia (with Michael Gilleland)
The Miracle of Language
More Anguished English
The Play of Words
Pun & Games
Puns Spooken Here (with P. C. Swanson)
Sleeping Dogs Don't Lay (with Richard Dowis)
The Wizard of Words
The Word Circus
Word Play Crosswards, volumes 1 and 2 (with Gayle Dean)
The Write Way (with Richard Dowis)

# The Cunning Linguist

Ribald Riddles,
Lascivious Limericks, Carnal Corn,
and Other Good, Clean Dirty Fun!

## Richard Lederer

Illustrated by Dave Morice

St. Martin's Griffin ✠ New York

www.stmartins.com

Library of Congress Cataloging-in-Publication Data

Lederer, Richard, 1938–
      The cunning linquist : ribald riddles, lascivious limericks, carnal corn, and other good, clean dirty fun! / Richard Lederer.
            p.   cm.
      ISBN 0-312-31813-8
            1. Sex—Humor.   I. Title.

PN6231.S54L394   2003
818'.5402—dc21

2003047160

First published in the United States by The Chicago Review Press under the title *Nothing Risqué, Nothing Gained*

First published in Great Britain by Robson

First St. Martin's Griffin Edition: December 2003

10  9  8  7  6  5  4  3  2  1

To my wife, Simone,
whose unwavering belief in this book
has made her filthy Rich

# Contents

A dirty mind is a terrible thing to waste.

# Acknowledgments

Thanks to Eric Albert, Douglas Fink, and David Shulman for some of the anagrams and Al Gregory for the British place-names in "Erotic English"; John Barry for the Sartre limerick, and Norman W. Storer for the title "A Leer of Limericks," and Don Hauptman and John Barry for their helpings of poonerisms.

And thank you, St. Martin's Press, for having the guts to publish the book with its intended title and for bringing its editor, Marian Lizzi, into my life.

# Author's Warning

- Who's the most popular man in the nudist colony?
  *The one who can carry two large coffees and a dozen donuts.*

- Who's the most popular woman in the nudist colony?
  *The one who can eat the last two donuts.*

You won't find jokes like these in this book. That's because *The Cunning Linguist* deals exclusively with sexual humor that depends on wordplay.

And that's not all that you won't find in the pages coming up. Absent are homosexual jokes, AIDS jokes, rape jokes, racial and religious jokes (well, just a few about priests and nuns), and jokes involving wildly aberrant sexual acts. I honestly believe that jokes should be obscene but not hurt.

What you will find in this book is a lot of good, clean dirty fun from the files of this cunning linguist. Most of the narratives and one-liners are about heterosexual intercourse, with a few other bodily activities and functions thrown in for good pleasure. You'll discover more than two thousand jokes and quickies that play with the verbal vivacity of our vocabulary and illustrate one of the most astonishing miracles of language—the ability of two or more meanings to occupy the same space at the same time. That so many tour de farces can combine one meaning that looks you straight in the eye with another that gives you a lewd wink is very much a part of that miracle.

Our greatest writers have been perpetrating this kind of handy-randy wordplay for centuries. Shakespeare used it when— to take one of tens of examples of the Bard's sexually organic humor—he had his mercurial Mercutio, in *Romeo and Juliet*, declaim, "The bawdy hand of the dial is on the prick of noon." (Not long after, Mercutio was run through by Tybalt, proving that in some cases the sword is mightier than the pun.)

Alexander Pope used it when he wrote in "The Rape of the Lock":

*Men prove with child, as powerful fancy works,*
*And maids, turned bottles, cry aloud for corks.*

Even in our classic children's literature such humor is par for the coarse. Don't think that Jonathan Swift was innocently unaware of the lewd, lecherous, lascivious, and licentious pun he embedded in the third paragraph of *Gulliver's Travels:* "But, my good *master Bates* dying in two years after, and I having few friends, my business began to fail" (emphasis mine).

While *The Cunning Linguist* could also have been titled *Filthy Rich* or *An Embarrassment of Rich's*, I trust that you will not be offended by the assorted sorta sordid sortees in this book. If you are easily shocked, stop reading right now and pass this collection on to someone among the 86.8 percent of the American population who enjoys such sexual shenanigans. Nobody is forcing your fingers to turn the pages or gluing your eyeballs to the print.

If you do decide to move on beyond this introduction, I'm confident that you'll gain a new respect for the procreative potentialities of the English language. You'll also experience the beneficial effects of protracted laughter.

Medieval physicians believed that the state of one's health was determined by a balance of mysterious fluids called "humors." Today, there is considerable evidence that humor, in the modern sense, is indeed a healer. As humor guru Joel Goodman once pointed out, "Seven days without laughter makes one weak."

One caution, though: Please, don't overdose by reading too much at one time. Jokes in their written form should be ingested slowly; I prescribe no more than two chapters per portion. Otherwise, you will find yourself suffering from premature joke elation.

This book is the loving labor of more than a half-century of collecting and filing. I may not look bluish, but I've probably spent the equivalent of three full years of my life trading dirty jokes with other connoisewers, sometimes by letter, usually in the position of a missionary—face-to-face. It's an activity that has given me a lot of pleasure, and I've written this book to add such pleasure to your life. After all, nothing risqué, nothing gained. A dirty mind is a terrible thing to waste.

Richard Lederer, San Diego
richard.lederer@pobox.com
www.verbivore.com

# Do You Have a Dirty Mind?

In a junior high-school biology class the teacher asks a student, "Mary, please name the part of the human body that expands to six times its normal size and explain under what conditions."

Blushing bright red, Mary simpers, "Teacher, that is not a proper question to ask me, and I can't answer it in front of the class."

The teacher turns to another student and asks, "All right, Johnny, do you have the answer?"

"The pupil of the eye, and in dim light."

"Correct. Now, Mary, I want to tell you three things. First, you didn't do your homework last night. Second, you have a dirty mind. And third, when you grow up, you're going to be dreadfully disappointed."

As you started reading the joke above, did you, like the crimson-faced Mary, assume that something lewd was going on? Does the fact that you have bought this book and have read past the introduction into this first chapter indicate that you, like Mary, have a dirty mind?

Are your thoughts squeaky clean or quietly filthy? To find out, take a crack at the twenty-five questions below. Then compare your answers with those that follow the list.

1. What's big and hairy and sticks out of a man's pajamas and is so big that he can hang his hat on it?

2. What does a man do standing up that a woman does sitting down and a dog does on three legs?

3. What does a cow have four of that a woman has only two of?

4. What goes in pink and stiff and comes out soft and squishy?

5. What is long and hard, has two nuts, and can make a woman smile and then regret that she has grown bigger?

6. What four-letter word ends with *k* and means "intercourse"?

7. What word starts with *c* and ends with *t* and means "pussy"?

8. What four-letter word ends in *it* and is found on the bottom of a birdcage?

9. What is a word that begins with *f* and ends with *uck*?

10. What four-letter word ends with *unt* and means "a female"?

11. What does a man have in his pocket that's about six inches long, has a head on it, and women love it so much they often blow it?

12. What is all wrinkled and hangs out your underpants?

13. What's a Spanish fly?

14. What does a dog do that a man steps into, and what does a dog make in the yard that a man wouldn't want to step into unexpectedly?

15. What do you do to an elephant with three balls?

What does a cow have four of
that a woman has only two of?

16. What kind of a man sticks his tool into another man's mouth?

17. What is long and hard and contains seamen?

18. What does a man have in his pants that you can also find on a pool table?

19. Where do women have the curliest hair?

20. What happened to the couple who didn't know the difference between Vaseline and putty?

21. I'm thinking of something that a man gives to a women after they're married. Solzhenitsyn has one of these and it's long and hard; George Bush has a little one; Madonna doesn't have one; and the Pope has one, but he doesn't use it. What am I thinking of?

22. What sticks out, comes in many sizes, drops when it isn't well, and feels better when you blow it?

23. What wasn't a maiden for long, especially after more than a thousand people went down with her?

24. What has a stiff shaft, penetrates at the tip, and comes with a quiver?

25. Why do policemen have bigger balls than firemen?

## ANSWERS

1. His head.

2. Shake hands.

3. Legs.

4. Chewing gum.

5. Almond Joy candy bar.

6. Talk.

7. Cat.

8. Grit.

9. Firetruck.

10. Aunt.

11. A dollar bill (or any other denomination of paper money).

12. Your mother.

13. A pop-up in a Madrid baseball game.

14. Pants. A hole.

15. Walk him and pitch to the giraffe.

16. A dentist.

17. A submarine.

18. Pockets.

19. Africa.

20. All their windows fell out.

21. A last name.

22. A nose.

23. The *Titanic*.

24. An arrow.

25. They sell more tickets.

# Punography

In the early eighteenth century a jeering-impaired playwright and critic named John Dennis scowled that a pun is the lowest form of wit. Two centuries later a fellow named Henry Erskine pun-upped him with "if a pun is the lowest form of wit, it is, therefore, the foundation of all wit."

The lowly pun is certainly the foundation of blue wit, as witness these punographic examples, all of which demonstrate that the pun is mightier than the sword, or that, as Mark Twain pointed out: The penis—mightier than the sword! Sharpen your pun cells, and let's get right to wit:

- The four stages of the typical couple's sex life:
  Under 35: Tri-weekly.
  35–45: Try weekly.
  45–55: Try weakly.
  55 and over: Try, try, try.

- If Guinevere gave Lancelot, I wonder how much Galahad.

- BRUTUS: "How many women did you have oral sex with last night, Caesar?"
  CAESAR: "Et tu, Brutus."

- Three old ladies went for a tramp in the woods—but he got away. Next morning they caught him, and for the rest of the day their stomachs were on the bum. Next day the three ladies were confronted by a flasher. The first had a stroke, and the second had a stroke—but the third wouldn't touch it.

- Tom's Dick is Harry.

- When they lose their jobs, priests are defrocked and lawyers are disbarred. When coquettes are fired, they are decoyed; when pornographers are fired, they are deluded; when models are fired, they are denuded and disposed; and when prostitutes are fired, they are detailed and delayed.

- Everyone has heard of Elvis the Pelvis, but few people know that he had a brother Enos.

- There's something about women that attracts me, and I'm trying to put my finger on it.

- This is a true story. In 1989 a Las Vegas whorehouse called the Mustang Ranch went into bankruptcy. For some months the U.S. government thought about taking over and running the place to recoup some of the debts, giving new meaning to the terms *belly up* and *going in the hole*.

- More true facts (you wouldn't want false facts, would you?): In Upper Manhattan, near the Cloisters, there is an intersection of two streets—Seamen and Cumming.

- The Masai tribe of Africa use cow manure as a cold cream for their complexions. Thus, the Masai get literally shit-faced.

- The biblical book of Exodus tells us, "Thou shalt not covet thy neighbor's house . . . nor his ass." In the Song of Solomon we read, "My beloved put in his hand by the hole of the door, and my bowels were moved for him."

- During the mid-nineteenth century, a French actor who called himself Le Petomane ("the Fartist") would gulp great quantities of air and then, at will, fart out songs. He gave new meaning to the term *wind instrument*.

- William Shakespeare's Bottom really made an ass of himself.

- While at vespers, a well-endowed nun discovers that her bra strap has broken. Embarrassed by the situation, she turns to the Mother Superior and blushes, "May I be excused, Mother? My cup runneth over."

- If Eve was created from Adam's rib, was Adam ribballed?

- "Balls!" said the queen. "If I had them, I'd be king!"

- Once a king, always a king, but once a knight's enough.

- Kotex isn't the best thing, but it's next to the best thing.

- If love and marriage go together like the horse and carriage, why do so many couples put the cart before the horse?

- You can't have your Kate and Edith too.

- Oh, give me a home where the buffalo roam, and the deer and the antelope play . . . and I'll show you a home filled with all kinds of shit.

- Women can make competent doctors—and they often do!

- Two women built and operated a small but efficient storage facility in Dallas. They ran the best little warehouse in Texas. Then they opened a marina—the best little oarhouse in Texas; then a rabbit farm—the best little harehouse in Texas. Finally they opened a theater that showed scary movies—the best little horror house in Texas.

- With fiends like you, who needs enemas?

- Down with pants! Up with miniskirts!

- The human race has multiplied not because of an apple in a tree but because of a pair in the grass.

- Little Jack Horner put his thumb in the pie and his finger in the tart—and Popeye dipped his finger in Olive Oyl.

- Try this one for a guaranteed laugh at a party. Present two people a card that reads:
First reader: HOOF HEARTED?
Second reader: ICE MELTED.

- For another surefire party laugh, ask someone to repeat this sentence rapidly five times: "One smart feller, he felt smart. . . ."

- I invite the men to try this one on the telephone: Ask a friend on the other end of the line, "What's ugly, has a half-inch penis, and hangs down?" If the friend doesn't know, answer, "A bat." Then ask, "What's handsome, has a ten-inch penis, and hangs up?" Before the friend can answer, hang up.

- Q. Got a match?
A. Yeah, my ass and your face.

- The other day I got hit in the nuts by a tennis ball. Ever since I've been feeling crotchety and testy.

- Nothing can replace the bikini—and it often does!

- We live in a crazy world. Turn the men upside down and they're all nuts. Turn the women upside down and they're all cracked. Turn them both upside down and they're all screwy.

- The apple of a man's eye is usually the prettiest peach with the biggest pear and the reddest cherry.

- My woman isn't complex. Anybody can grasp her.

- Most women don't like to sleep on their stomachs—and most men do. And remember: if you don't want to sleep on a full stomach, don't feed her.

- Did you know that many secretaries are unsuited for their work?

- F-U-C-K, tell her I want her.

- Man to woman: "Let's get something straight between us."

- When a man has everything he wants in a woman—it is!

- A sultan was inspecting the quarters of his harem. He opened a closet in one of the bedrooms and let out a terrified sheik.

- Two female nudists were strolling through the colony when one asked, "Is that Dick Brown over there?" Replied the second: "It should be. He's been here for three weeks."

- An eighty-year-old man who had proclivities toward exhibitionism was arrested for displaying his dried arrangement. When he tried to force himself on a young woman, he was booked again for assault with a dead weapon.

- Thieves stole all the toilets from a police station. The cops never were able to solve the case because they didn't have anything to go on.

- SHE: "Don't you know what good clean fun is?"
  HE: "No, what good is it?"

- Sign in a public bathroom: "Remember: The job is never finished until the paperwork is done!"

- Sign at a public pool: "OOL: You'll note that there's no pee in our pool. Please keep it that way."

- Sign in a public men's lavatory: "We aim to please. Won't you aim too, please?"

- Sign on a small lamp affixed to a tile wall just above a public urinal: "Let this be a light to lighten the genitals."

- Road signs are often prophetic. For example:
  SOFT SHOULDERS
  DANGEROUS CURVES
  MERGING TRAFFIC

"Don't you know what good clean fun is?"

MEN AT WORK
LOOK OUT FOR CHILDREN

- The Democratic Party is considering changing its emblem from a donkey to a condom because it expands with inflation, limits productivity, encourages cooperation, and gives you a feeling of security, although you know you're getting screwed.

- Then there's the wife who received a postcard from her husband, who was away on a business trip: "Having a wonderful time, darling. Wish you were her."

- Genitals prefer blondes.

- Women have been known to raise their hems to get their hims.

- Love thy neighbor—but don't get caught!

- T-shirt message in New Orleans:
  Shuck me.
  Suck me.
  Eat me raw.

- Give a woman an inch, and she thinks she's a ruler.

- The trouble with most women is most men.

- There's a new book out that contains death notices of famous men and women. It's called *Obituaries*. The author is writing a sequel. It's called *Son of Obituaries*.

- 2 skins + 2 skins = 4 skins. 2 Q + 2 Q = 4 Q.

- HUSBAND: "I want to make love with you in the worst way." WIFE: "You've been doing that for years!"

- One of America's greatest technology universities, MIT, has opened a branch in South Hampton.

- My knowledge of sexual humor may not be vast, but it is half vast.

- FIRST MAN: "I took a vacation to Florida."
  SECOND MAN: "Tampa with your girlfriend?"
  FIRST MAN: "I sure did—again and again!"
  SECOND MAN: "Well, my girlfriend and I went to the Caribbean, and we made love three times a day."
  FIRST MAN: "Jamaica?"
  SECOND MAN: "No, she did it quite voluntarily."
  FIRST MAN: "Then we traveled to the Pacific."
  SECOND MAN: "Samoa?"
  FIRST MAN: "Yep, she gave me samoa."

- This reputedly happened on *The Newlywed Game:* The new groom was asked the weirdest place that the couple ever made whoopie. With confidence he replied, "Got to be the butt, Bob."

- Women went wild over the professional stud because they liked the way his balls would jiggle low.

- Early American pioneers always knew the lay of the land—and just where to find her.

- A very short man was dancing with a very tall woman. He propositioned her, and all he got was a bust in the mouth. Eventually he went to bed with the woman, but his friends had to put him up to it.

- Last knight a bishop got rooked by a queen haw-king pawn.

- A boy who was the product of artificial insemination grew up to be completely unmanageable. The moral: Spare the rod and spoil the child.

- When I travel on an airplane, I like to be served TWA milk and TWA coffee. But I love to be served TWA tea.

- A nymphomaniac in Mexico is a señor-eater. In Israel she's a Heblew, and in Alaska a snowblower.

- Speaking of oral sex, many an Arab has gone out into the desert to eat dates and then to throw in some nuts.

- Many an octogenarian has had an out-of-body experience. In fact, they've been out of body experiences for a long time.

- SHE: "Aren't the stars lovely tonight?"
HE: "Are they? I'm in no position to say."

- When it comes to women, the double-breasted look will always be in.

- Women who do aerobics have legs like this: ! !
Women who get drunk have legs like this: ) (
Women who screw around a lot have legs like this: ( )
Women who learn to just say no have legs like this: X

- Title of a new movie about sex videos distributed at no charge: *Porn Free.*

- "I've been constipated for the past two weeks."
"No shit?"

- HE [at a drugstore counter]: "Can I have a dozen condoms, miss?"
SHE: "Don't miss me, mister!"
HE: "Well then, you better make it thirteen."

- Did you know that absinthe makes the tart grow fonder?

- Male jogger catching up to an attractive and bouncy female jogger: "My pace or yours?"

- I often feel like a twenty-year-old, but I seldom can find one.

- Don't criticize nudists. They were born that way.

- When you visit Philadelphia, be sure to look up my girlfriend.

- In my dream I was at an Internet café when my server went down on me.

- I got a sweater for Christmas. I really wanted a screamer or a moaner.

- Food has replaced sex in my life. Now I can't even get into my own pants.

- What's all the fuss about same-sex marriages? I've been married for years, and I keep having the same sex.

- Sex is a lot like doing laundry. If you have a small load, do it by hand.

- I got caught stealing rubbers and they treated me like a condom criminal.

- Seven dwarfs sat in the tub, feeling Happy. Then Happy got out, so they all felt Grumpy.

- There was a fire in the boardinghouse where all the chorus girls from a nearby burlesque theater stayed during show runs.
  It took firemen three hours to put the fire out.
  Then it took the police three more hours to put the firemen out.

- Being old is like being an army sergeant. Most of the time you're trying to get your privates to stand at attention.

- Men are like floor tiles. If you lay them properly the first time, you can walk all over them for life.

- Men are like chocolate bars—sweet, smooth, and they usually go right to your hips.

- It takes many nails to build a crib, but it only takes one screw to fill it.

- I love oral sex. It's the phone bill I hate.

- I used to be a Scrabble champion, but I became inconsonant, and now I can't move my vowels.

- A guy walks into the psychiatrist's office wearing only underwear made from Saran Wrap. The psychiatrist says, "Well, I can clearly see you're nuts."

- An employer gave his secretary a dress for her first week's salary. The next week, he raised her salary.

- I make music using a pair of metallic dildos. Yep, phallic cymbals.

- Let me assure you that sex over sixty can indeed be both deadly and very dangerous. I strongly recommend obeying the speed limit.

- Ninety-five percent of all people have hemorrhoids. The other 5 percent are perfect assholes.

- People who say that they don't fart are probably full of hot air.

- The most recent survey on women showed that 10 percent of the men interviewed liked women with thin legs. Another 15 percent preferred muscular legs. The rest liked something in-between.

- A young woman participating in a survey was asked how she felt about condoms. She answered, "Well, that depends on what's in it for me."

- Sex is like a bridge game. You don't need a partner if you have a good hand.

- Men who make obscene phone calls have sexual hang-ups.

- Mahoney: "I haven't been feelin' meself lately!"
  O'Reilly: " 'Tis a good thing, too. That was a nasty habit you had!"

- I know a guy who plays it so safe that he wears rubbers even during oral sex. Twice a week his girlfriend blows him to condom come.

- A judge kept ruling that no pornographic movie could be offered on the market. Several enraged porn actors and actresses ganged up on him in a dark alley and choked his honor to death. Ever since he's been known as the star-strangled banner.

## Bedroom Golf

1. The player will furnish his own equipment for play, normally one club and two balls.

2. Owner of the course must approve equipment before play can begin.

3. Unlike regular golf, the object of the game is to get the club into the hole while keeping the balls out and to take as many strokes as possible until the course owner is satisfied.

4. For most effective play, the club should have a firm shaft. The owner of the course may check the stiffness of the shaft before allowing play to commence.

5. Long drives and putts are especially admired.

6. Course owner reserves the right to restrict the length of shaft so as to avoid damage to the course.

7. Players are cautioned to play the correct hole, as indicated by the course owner, and to refrain from mentioning to the owner of the course currently being played other courses they have recently toured.

8. It is considered bad form to begin playing the hole immediately upon arrival at the course. Experienced players will admire the course, paying special attention to the well-formed bunkers, and then commence a lengthy foreplay.

9. It is considered outstanding form to play the hole several times in one match.

10. It is considered bad form to reveal your score to other players, or even that you have played the course.


• I heard a joke that's so funny you'll laugh your tits right off. Oh . . . you've already heard it.

- HE: "Would you like to have mutual orgasm?"
  SHE: "No, I'm perfectly happy with State Farm."

- When Jimmy Carter won election as president, a lot of his opponents experienced peanut envy.

- A woman who puts out often puts in.

- Have you heard that Xerox and Wurlitzer have just merged? They're going to manufacture reproductive organs.

- Have a Merry Syphilis and a Happy Gonorrhea.

- Nothing succeeds like excess.

- It's better to be pissed off than pissed on.

- Schlong. Gotta beat it.

# Sexicography

Dictionaries have been around for more than two thousand years, going back at least to ancient Greece. Today's wordbooks are designed for many different audiences, ranging from picture dictionaries for small children to highly specialized technical lexicons, from palm-sized pocket dictionaries to big, fat, unabridged volumes like the *Oxford English Dictionary*, which defines more than 615,000 words. Some of these words are of the four-letter variety.

An elderly lady once chastised a librarian for having an unabridged dictionary with such "naughty words" on open display in a public library. The librarian replied, "Madam, you would not even know that such words are in the dictionary unless you had looked them up."

Why plow through the dictionary looking for the definitions of scattered "naughty words" when you can use the compact, irreverent glossary in this chapter? Why look up the unembellished, boring denotations of words and phrases when you can discover their lewdly suggestive connotations in one handy sex-icon? It is high time to add to the long and glorious tradition of lexicography by compiling a new collection of definitions—*The Dirty Dicktionary:*

- *adolescence.* The time of life between childhood and adultery.
- *alimony.* The billing without the cooing. The screwing you get for the screwing you got.
- *analogy.* The study of assholes.
- *anthole.* Where an uncle likes to come.
- *artificial insemination.* Impregnation without representation.
- *asphalt.* Hemorrhoids.
- *aspic.* Rectal scratching.
- *asshole.* A rest room inconveniently located right next to a snack bar.
- *athletic supporter.* A fan who bangs the whole team.
- *atitter.* A breast man.
- *backdoor approach.* A position taken by a man who likes to come with her tail between his legs.
- *balderdash.* Screw-and-run.
- *ballbuster.* A nutcracker sweet.
- *balled.* Getting more head than other men.
- *balsam.* To screw around a little.
- *bathing beauty.* A woman worth wading for.
- *birth control.* An issue that attempts to avoid the issue.
- *blow job.* Lip service.
- *blueprints.* Dirty films.
- *blunderbus.* A baby carriage.
- *bottom dollar.* Fee that a prostitute charges.

- *bottoms up!* Doggy-style sex.

- *braless.* Having no invisible means of support.

- *brassiere.* An over-the-shoulder boulder holder. A booby trap.

- *brave.* A cannibal who lets his wife give him head.

- *broadcasting.* Fishing for women.

- *buggerer.* A fanny farmer.

- *buttressed.* A comfortable reclining chair.

- *canopy.* Urine specimen.

- *card.* A jack ace who ought to be dealt with.

- *chastity belt.* A labor-saving device.

- *cherry float.* A virgin on a water bed.

- *chestnut.* A man who loves topless dancers.

- *circle jerk.* A group of people who pull themselves together.

- *claptrap.* A prophylactic.

- *cleavage.* Valley of the dolls.

- *cobra.* An article of apparel worn by female Siamese twins.

- *cockpit.* A vagina.

- *cocktail party.* An affair where a man gets stiff, a woman gets tight, and they return home to find that neither is either.

- *coitus.* A serpent in paradise.

- *condiment.* A flavored confection shaped like an erection.

- *condominium.* Where people who want to have safe sex live.

- *continental breakfast.* A roll in bed with some honey.

- *contraceptive.* An article to be worn on every conceivable occasion.

- *contraceptive gel.* The sperminator.
- *coolie.* A quickie on a ski lift.
- *cooperates.* She coos and he operates.
- *cuckold.* Somebody that somebody else really has it in for.
- *cunnilingus.* Getting one's licks in. A real tongue twister.
- *dancing.* A vertical expression for horizontal intention. A navel engagement with no discharge of semen.
- *decaffeinated.* What a cow gets when it has a baby.
- *diaper.* A bum wrap.
- *diaphragm.* A trampoline for a schmuck. An immaculate contraception.
- *diarrhea.* At loose ends.
- *dictator.* A vegetable dildo.
- *dildo.* A meat substitute.
- *dishonorable discharge.* What happens after he says, "I won't come in your mouth."
- *donuts.* No such thing. Only bucks have them.
- *dork.* A pig's dick.
- *drive-in movie.* Wall-to-wall car petting.
- *egghead.* What Mrs. Dumpty gives to Humpty.
- *election.* Japanese hard-on.
- *elixir.* What an amorous man sometimes does to a woman.
- *elliptical.* A kiss.
- *erection.* Voting day in Tokyo.
- *eternity.* The length of time between when you come and she leaves.
- *eucalyptus.* What babies would say to their moels.

- *eunuch*. A man who is fixed for life and has nothing more to lose, who hasn't got the balls to give someone else the shaft, and who has no nuts and no dates.

- *European*. What you're a-doin' in the john.

- *executrix*. A call girl for CEOs.

- *exhibitionist*. A fellow who lets it all hang out.

- *falsies*. Making mountains out of molehills.

- *fantasizing*. Baring somebody else in mind.

- *fast woman*. One who goes from zero to sixty-nine in under fifteen seconds.

- *fellatio*. A taste of things to come.

- *flatbush*. What a woman gets when she wears tight jeans.

- *foot fetish*. What a woman has when she's never satisfied with anything less than twelve inches.

- *foreplay*. Intercourse behind the bush growing next to the first hole.

- *Freudian slip*. What Sigmund tried to remove from his wife each night.

- *frigidity*. Not giving a fuck.

- *frigid woman*. An ice cube with a hole in it.

- *full moon*. What your repairman reveals when he bends over to fix your fridge.

- *fungi*. A male mushroom with a ten-inch root.

- *gastric*. A cleverly timed fart.

- *gold digger*. A fund-lover who can extract a pearl from a nut and a Persian lamb from an old goat. A woman who doesn't like a man's company unless he owns it.

- *golden fleece*. What all of King Midas's women had.

- *gourmet blow job*. When someone eats you under the table.

- *grasshopper*. A man who can't afford to screw in a motel.
- *grass widow*. A woman who isn't necessarily green.
- *gynecologist*. A spreader of old wives' tails.
- *hard-on*. An up-and-coming standout with a swelled head and a stiff neck. A rising to the occasion.
- *headrest*. A break between two oral sex sessions.
- *hermit*. A guy who likes to get off by himself.
- *high-minded*. Believing that the way to a man's heart is through his stomach.
- *honeymoon*. The tail end of a wedding.
- *honeymooner*. A bee who drops his pants.
- *horizon*. A prostitute getting out of bed.
- *hors de combat*. Camp followers.
- *hospice*. Equine urine.
- *husband*. A rake that has been converted to a lawn mower.
- *impede*. Gnome urinated.
- *impotence*. When your organ gives out on your favorite piece. Nature's way of saying, "No hard feelings." Long time no seed.
- *indecent, infirm, ingrate*. Big enough, long enough, and hard enough.
- *indifferent*. Anal sex.
- *infatuation*. Dame foolishness.
- *innuendo*. An Italian suppository.
- *intercourse*. An injection of affection from a projection to the midsection without objection. A new direction for a nude erection. Invasion of the body snatch.
- *intuit*. What a penis likes to get.
- *jitterbugger*. A nervous sex maniac.

Honeymooner

- *kissing.* An application for a better position. Uptown shopping for downtown business. An upper persuasion for lower invasion.

- *lickety-split.* The speed limit on Highway 69.

- *life.* A sexually transmitted disease that spans the time between the womb and the tomb, the sperm and the worm, the erection and the resurrection.

- *limp.* The state of a backward glans.

- *loggerheads.* Toilets for lumberjacks.

- *loose woman.* One more to be petted than censured.

- *loosey-goosey.* A fowl with diarrhea.

- *LP.* Spanish urine.

- *male stripper.* One who is unsuited for his job.

- *man.* A life-support system for a penis.

- *marriage.* A spouse trap.

- *marriage license.* A noose paper.

- *masturbation.* Taking your life into your own hands. Holding your own. Pulling a boner. Getting a good grip on yourself. Romancing the bone. The sin of emission. Touch and go. An act that comes in handy.

- *masturbator.* A champion fisherman who believes that a bird in the hand is worth two in the bush.

- *maternity dress.* A slip cover.

- *ménage à trois.* A triangle that often results in a wrecktangle.

- *menstruation.* A bloody waste of fucking time.

- *meteorologist.* A corpulent piss-doctor.

- *miniskirt.* So little raised so high to reveal so much that needs cover so badly.

- *minuteman.* A guy who double-parks in front of a whore-house.

- *mistress.* Someone who's halfway between a mister and a mat-tress.

- *molasses.* The back part of moles.

- *morass.* What everybody wants.

- *mustache.* A womb broom.

- *nervous man.* One who has a wife, girlfriend, and bank note, all three months overdue.

- *New England.* Upper U.S.

- *nudism.* Making a clean breast of things.

- *nudist.* A buff buff that you just have to bare with, who is wrapped up only in himself, on whom nothing looks good, who puts on air, who grins and bares it, and who wears a one-button suit.

- *nudist camp.* A place where men and women air their differ-ences, bare with each other, live life in the raw, greet each dawn as a nude day, and are all together in the altogether. To join, just leave your name and dress.

- *nymphomania.* An ailment in which the patient enjoys being bedridden.

- *nymphomaniac.* Piece on earth, good will to men.

- *oar.* A cockney prostitute.

- *old age.* When it takes you all night to do what you used to do all night.

- *oral contraceptives.* Screw pills.

- *oral sex.* Getting your licks in.

- *orgasm.* A spasm in a chasm.

- *padded bra.* A false front.

- *panhandler*. What Tinkerbell wants to be.
- *passion play*. First move on a date.
- *pathetic fallacy*. A small pecker.
- *pecan*. A bedpan.
- *Peeping Tom*. A man with an overdose of vitamin see.
- *penis*. The only thing that a woman hopes she will find hard to handle. What a man wants most in a woman.
- *Peter Pan*. A basin under a hospital bed.
- *pièce de résistance*. An underground nymphomaniac.
- *piece of ass*. What everybody gets at a donkey roast.
- *pith*. What you take when you drink too much thoda.
- *playboy*. A man who keeps coming and going.
- *poppycock*. What a mommy loves to take in at night.
- *pop quiz*. A paternity suit.
- *porno filmmaker*. A crack photographer.
- *prediction*. Foreplay.
- *premature ejaculation*. Touch and go.
- *prickly heat*. What causes erections.
- *private tutor*. One who doesn't fart in public.
- *prophylactic*. A rubber check.
- *prostate*. What causes older men to get up in the wee wee hours of the morning.
- *prostitute*. Bang for the buck. A woman who makes her living being laid back but who is always pressed for cash.
- *ramification*. What made Mary have a little lamb.
- *ratchet*. Rodent feces.
- *ray*. Japanese intercourse.

- *romantic setting.* One with a diamond in it.
- *satyriasis.* Penal servitude.
- *screwball.* Dance at a bordello.
- *screwdriver.* A pimp.
- *seersucker.* A person who blows clairvoyants.
- *semen.* A drip off the old cock.
- *serenity.* A building that houses a sorority and a fraternity.
- *seven-up.* Sex with Snow White.
- *sex education.* Sermon on the mount.
- *sexual revolution.* Copulation explosion.
- *shampoo.* The plastic mounds of dog shit that you can buy in novelty stores. Related to cacaphony.
- *shortcoming.* Premature ejaculation.
- *silicone treatment.* The bust that money can buy.
- *sinecure.* Treatment for VD.
- *smart woman.* Somebody who holds a man at arm's length but doesn't lose her grip on him.
- *sodomist.* Somebody who likes to come from behind.
- *software.* Condoms for old men.
- *spooning.* What comes immediately before forking.
- *stalemate.* A lover who has grown predictable in bed.
- *stripling.* A burlesque princess.
- *strip poker.* A game in which the more you lose the more you have to show for it.
- *subpoena.* From the root *sub,* "below," and the Latin *poena,* "male." Therefore, "below the penis," or, "by the balls."
- *surfeit.* A vagina.
- *surtax.* An extra charge at a whorehouse.

- *syntax*. Venereal disease.
- *tear jerker*. A man who cries while he masturbates.
- *teepee*. Urine produced by drinking too much tea.
- *testicles*. How to find out if a man is ticklish.
- *toilet tissue*. Crapping paper.
- *tool kit*. A box of dildos.
- *transistor*. A cross-dressing nun.
- *trapeze*. What toilet bowls do.
- *twin*. A womb-mate.
- *unique*. A nutless Frenchman.
- *vagina*. A balled spot. The box a cock comes in.
- *vampire*. A conflagration of seductive women.
- *vasectomy*. Never having to say you're sorry.
- *Vaseline*. An ointment ensuring that love is never having to say you're sore.
- *venereal disease*. Germs of endearment.
- *vibrators*. Toys for twats.
- *vice versa*. Dirty Italian poetry.
- *virgin*. A woman born but not made. Someone who doesn't give a fuck.
- *voyeurs*. People who need peepholes.
- *wholesale*. Bargain day at the whorehouse.
- *whore*. An undercover worker.
- *whorehouse*. A business dedicated to making sure the customer always comes first.
- *wife*. An attachment you screw on the bed to get the housework done.
- *wild goose*. A finger that's one inch off center.

- *wild oats*. Seeds sown by young lovers with the hope of crop failure.

- *wolf*. A man who always puts out a welcome mattress.

- *woman*. A life-support system for a vagina.

- *womb*. The sound of an elephant fart.

- *Yankee*. Same as a quickie, except that a guy can do it himself.

# Keep Your Pecker Up

*My nookie days are over. My pilot light is out.*
*What used to be my sex appeal is now my water*
   *spout.*
*Time was when, of its own accord, from my trousers*
   *it would spring,*
*But now I have a full-time job to find the blasted*
   *thing.*
*It used to be embarrassing the way it would behave,*
*For every single morning it would stand and watch*
   *me shave.*
*As my old age approaches, it sure gives me the blues*
*To see it hang its little head and watch me tie my shoes.*

The *it*, of course, is the baby-maker, banana, beard splitter, beef injection, boner, cock, crank, dick, dink, dipstick, dong, dork, eleventh finger, johnson, joystick, love muscle, meat, monkey, one-eyed mouse, pecker, prick, pud, putz, rod, root, schlong, schmuck, turkey neck, whang, willie—the penis by many other names.

- What did one ovary say to the other?
  *"Did you order any furniture? There's two nuts outside trying to shove an organ in."*

- How is a dick like fishing?
  *Throw back the small ones, eat the medium ones, and mount the large ones.*

- How is life like a penis?
  *When it's soft, you can't beat it, and when it's hard, you get screwed.*

- A secretary goes into her boss's office and asks, "May I use your Dictaphone?"
  He replies, "No. Use your finger like everyone else."

- I wish I could talk to my doctor about erectile dysfunction, but for some reason it never comes up.

- How do you spot the blind man at a nudist colony?
  *It isn't hard.*

- Why is a virgin like a balloon?
  *One prick and it's all over.*

- What did the sign on the door of the whorehouse say?
  *Beat it—we're closed.*

- How do you keep a hard-on?
  *Don't fuck with it.*

- What's the nicest thing about a nudist wedding?
  *You don't have to ask. You can see who the best man is.*

- What do a coffin and a condom have in common?
  *They're both filled with stiffs, but you come in one and go in the other.*

- Acupuncturists do it with a small prick.

- What is the lightest thing in the world?
  *A penis. Even a thought can raise it.*


When it comes to dirty humor many of us are caught in penal servitude, and we love to exchange jokes and verses about the male organ.

It isn't easy being a pecker these days. You've got a head you can't think with and only one eye, which you can't see out of.

You have to hang around with two nuts all the time, your closest neighbor is an asshole, and your best friend is a pussy.

Your owner beats you all the time, and now, because of AIDS, you have to wear a rubber diving suit.

When I was a kid, we used to recite this little ditty:

> *In days of old, when knights were bold,*
> *And rubbers weren't invented,*
> *They tied a sock around their cock,*
> *And babies were prevented.*

Nowadays, rubbers have been invented, and with increasing concern about AIDS and other sexually carried diseases, the U.S. government has created a National Condom Week. A contest was held soliciting snappy slogans that encourage the United States to become a condom nation. Here are the finalists:

- Cover your stump before you hump.
- Life is sweeter when you swaddle your peter.
- Before you attack her, wrap your whacker.
- Before you bag her, sheathe your dagger.
- A pike with armor will never harm her.
- If you can't seal your pecker, don't do more than neck her.
- Don't be nuts. Swaddle your putz.

- When in doubt, shroud your spout.
- She won't get sick if you wrap your dick.
- When you're in a jiffy, cover your stiffy.
- Bury your root before it's a shoot.
- Don't be a loner. Encase your boner.
- You can't go wrong if you shield your dong.
- If you're not going to sack it, go home and whack it.
- Don't pass go till your dork you stow.
- The best lover is undercover.
- Provide protection for your hot beef injection.
- If you like her spunky, cage your monkey.
- Provide a house for your one-eyed mouse.
- Before you bang, insulate your whang.
- Don't be silly. Protect your willy.
- When you undress Venus, dress your penis.
- Even when it's not December, be sure to gift wrap your member.
- Never deck her with an unwrapped pecker.
- Don't be a fool. Vulcanize your tool.
- The right selection: protect your erection.
- Wrap your dipstick in foil before checking her oil.
- If you really love her, wear a cover.
- Don't make a mistake. Muzzle your snake.
- When you go into heat, package your meat.
- Sex is cleaner with a kosher-wrapped wiener.
- Between her thighs, condomize.
- Seal your probe when you disrobe.

If you really love her, wear a cover.

- Before entering her socket, pocket your rocket.
- Women give thanks for rubberized cranks.
- Mute your trumpet before you hump it.
- Your mate you won't harrow if you quiver your arrow.
- A night in armor will never harm her.
- No glove—no love!

In summary, you gotta watch out for those germs of endearment because there's no such thing as an immaculate infection. So here's my advice to cocksure men: If you refuse to use condoms when having sex with a stranger, you are an asterisk it. Remember that flies carry germs—so keep yours closed. And to women: The love bug'll get you if you don't wash out!

## *Pro Boner*

- Have you heard about the new liquid Viagra? You simply go home and pour yourself a stiff one.
- Warning! A Viagra computer virus turns your floppy disk into a hard drive.
- What do Disney World and Viagra have in common? *They both make you wait an hour for a two-minute ride.*
- In pharmacology, all drugs have a generic name: Tylenol is acetaminophen, Aleve is naproxen, Amoxil is amoxicillin, Advil is ibuprofen, and so on. The FDA has been looking for a generic name for Viagra and announced that it has settled on mycoxafloppin. Also considered were mycoxafailin, mydixadrupin, mydixarizin, mydixadud, dixafix, ibepokin, and mount 'n' do.
- Prozac and Viagra. You come but you don't care where.
- It has come to the attention of researchers that a previously unanticipated reaction results when Viagra is taken along with

Ex-Lax. Both products tend to act together and magnify the effects of the other. The end result is that you end up both coming and going at the same time.

- Two Viagra pills walk into a bar and sit next to two marijuana plants. The marijuana plants are lamenting about being illegal. The Viagra pills scoff at them. One marijuana plant turns to the pills and asks, "Don't you think we should be legal?" "No," the Viagra pills say. "We're hard on drugs."

- What if the advertising agencies for other products came up with slogans for Viagra?:

- Viagra: It's "Whaazzzzz Up!"

- Viagra: The quicker pecker upper.

- Viagra: Like a rock!

- Viagra: When it absolutely, positively has to be there tonight.

- Viagra: Be all that you can be.

- Viagra: Reach out and touch someone.

- Viagra: Strong enough for a woman, but made for a man.

- Viagra: Tastes great! More filling!

- Viagra: We bring good things to life!

- This is your penis. This is your penis on drugs. Any questions?

## I Need a Raise

I, the penis, hereby request a raise in salary for the following reasons:

- I do physical labor.
- I work at great depths.
- I work headfirst.
- I do not get weekends off or public holidays.

- I work in a damp environment.

- I don't get paid overtime or shift penalties.

- I work in a dark workplace that has poor ventilation.

- I work in high temperatures.

- My work exposes me to contagious diseases.

Response from the administration:

After assessing your request, and considering the arguments you have raised, the administration rejects your request for the following reasons:

- You do not work eight hours straight. Who are you kidding?

- You fall asleep on the job after brief work periods.

- You do not always follow the orders of the management team.

- You do not stay in your allocated position, and often visit other areas.

- You take a lot of non-rostered breaks.

- You do not take initiative. You need to be pressured and stimulated in order to start working.

- You leave the workplace rather messy at the end of your shift.

- You don't always observe safety measures, such as wearing the correct protective outfits.

- You don't wait till pension age before retiring.

- You don't like working double shifts.

- You sometimes leave your allocated position before you have completed the day's work.

- And if that were not all, you have been seen constantly entering and leaving the workplace carrying two suspicious looking bags.

# The Pecker Tax

TO:        All Male Taxpayers
FROM:      The Internal Revenue Service
SUBJECT:   Revenue Enhancement

Dear Taxpayer:

The only thing that the Internal Revenue Service has not taxed to date is your penis. This is because 40 percent of the time it is hanging around unemployed, 30 percent of the time it is pissed off, 20 percent of the time it is hard up, and 10 percent of the time it is employed but operates in the hole. Furthermore, it has two testy descendants who are nuts.

Accordingly, after January 1, 2004, your pecker will be taxed according to its size. Using the "Pecker-Checker Schedule" below, determine your category and fill in the additional tax figure under "Other Taxes" on Page 8, Part XIV, line 36 of your Standard Income Tax Return (Form 1040 or 1040A).

## PECKER-CHECKER SCHEDULE

| 11 to 12 inches | Capital Gains Tax | $300.00 |
|---|---|---|
| 9 to 10 inches | Luxury Tax | $200.00 |
| 7 to 8 inches | Exercise Tax | $100.00 |
| 5 to 6 inches | Pole Tax | $50.00 |
| 3 to 4 inches | Nuisance Tax | $25.00 |

NOTE: Anyone under three (3) inches will be eligible for a refund. Do not apply for an extension.

Sincerely,
*Will I. Kutchapeckeroff*
*IRS Peckertaxer*

## Measure for Measure

A theater company comes into a small town to perform a series of Shakespeare plays. The company publicist attempts to place the names of the works on the marquee of the town theater, but it's too small and the titles don't fit.

The publicist knows that the citizenry of the town is especially knowledgeable about Shakespearean drama, so that afternoon the following shorthand appears on the marquee:

| | |
|---|---|
| • 2 inches | • 14 inches |
| • 4 inches | • wet |
| • 6 inches | • dry |
| • 8 inches | • masturbation |
| • 10 inches | • orgasm |
| • 12 inches | |

And the townspeople, being hip to the Bard, know exactly what Shakespeare plays are going to be performed:

| | |
|---|---|
| • 2 inches | *Much Ado About Nothing* |
| • 4 inches | *The Comedy of Errors* |
| • 6 inches | *As You Like It* |
| • 8 inches | *The Tempest* |
| • 10 inches | *The Taming of the Shrew* |
| • 12 inches | *The Merry Wives of Windsor* |
| • 14 inches | *Two Gentlemen of Verona* |
| • wet | *Midsummer Night's Dream* |
| • dry | *Twelfth Night* |
| • masturbation | *Love's Labor's Lost* |
| • orgasm | *All's Well That Ends Well* |

## The Great Debate

The parts of the body become engaged in a heated debate about which of them has the toughest job. After a while, Ms. Stomach gets the attention of her fellow organs and body parts: "Surely you will agree that among us it is I who have to bear the brunt of responsibility and hard work. All day long the pizza, the potato chips, and the soft drinks are dumped on me, and I have to sort out the good stuff for the fuel that runs the entire operation and send the waste on to that guy over there, Mr. Asshole."

There is general agreement that Ms. Stomach has the toughest job until the Feet twins take the floor: "How about us? We're the ones who support all the rest of you. We're the ones who get jammed into smelly old socks and get tied up in shoes that are too tight. And we get calluses and bunions because—bam! bam! bam!—we get stepped on all day long."

"Hear! Hear!" the other body parts fall into line. "Clearly it's the Feet twins that have the hardest job," they chorus.

Just then Mr. Penis stands up. "It's me, guys. I'm the one that goes through more hell than any of you."

"You, you crazy peckerhead? You must be nuts!" rejoin the other members.

"Yeah, me. How would you like it if they woke you up in the middle of the night, put a bag over your head, forced you into a dark, damp cave, and then made you do push-ups until you threw up?"

There is one last part to this story. The asshole enters the debate claiming that it has the toughest job. The other body parts refuse to listen, so the asshole closes up. The stomach, the feet, the pecker, and all the other organs, members, and appendages get deathly ill. Finally, they all have to admit that the asshole is the most important.

Moral: Every boss is an asshole.

## Pass the Word

A woman is helping her computer-illiterate husband set up his computer. At the appropriate point in the process, she tells him that he will now need to choose and enter a password to log on.

The husband is in a rather amorous mood and figures he will try for the shock effect. So when the computer asks him to enter his password, he makes it plainly obvious to his wife that he is keying in *penis*.

His wife falls off her chair laughing when the computer replies: PASSWORD REJECTED. NOT LONG ENOUGH.

# Bestiality

For twenty years a beech tree and a birch tree live next to each other in the woods. They coexist quite harmoniously until one day a sapling grows up in between them. The two trees get into a furious argument about whose offspring the little tree is.

"It's mine!" screams the beech.

"No, it's mine!" retorts the birch hatefully, and their argument echoes through the woods.

Then a woodpecker alights on the sapling and begins pecking away. "Oh, goody," say the beech tree and the birch tree. "Woodpeckers have sensitive beaks, so this guy will be able to settle our dispute. Mr. Woodpecker, pardon us, but can you tell us which of us trees is the parent of the sapling you're dining upon?"

"Well," muses the woodpecker, "I can't tell you if it's a son of a beech or a son of a birch, but it sure as hell is the best piece of ash I've ever stuck my pecker into!"

We know that human beings are descended from the animals

because the first ten years in a man's sex life he goes ape, gooses everything in sight, and crows about it; the next ten years he acts like a turkey and monkeys around; the next ten he spends lion about his abilities in the bedroom; and for all the rest he makes an ass of himself.

Perhaps because sex often brings out the animal and the beast in us, many jokes have as main characters our fellow creatures who run and creep and crawl and fly across the face of our planet. Related to fables, these tail tales often play up the particular characteristics of their bestial subjects.

## Strike It Rich

A buzzard, a turtle, and a rabbit pool their interests and acquire a good-sized farm. They begin to dig but realize that they have forgotten to buy fertilizer. Say the buzzard and the turtle to the rabbit, "You're the fastest of us, so you run to town for the manure."

Off speeds the rabbit, but it takes him three weeks to drag a huge sack of fertilizer back to the farm.

Meanwhile, the buzzard and turtle strike oil on their land. The resulting gusher makes a profit of millions, and the rabbit returns to a swank mansion surrounded by beautifully manicured grounds and flowing fountains. The rabbit hauls the sack to the front door and rings the bell. In a moment he's greeted by a butler in elegant attire.

"I'd like to know where my partners are, if that's not too much trouble. Where's the buzzard?" inquires the rabbit.

"Mr. BuzZARD is out in the yard," announces the butler.

"And where's the turtle?"

"Mr. TurTELL is out at the well."

"Is that so?" snaps the tuckered-out rabbit. "Well you can tell Mr. BuzZARD, who's out in the yard, and Mr. TurTELL, who's out at the well, that Mr. RabBIT is back with the shit!"

## A Whale of a Tale

Willy the Whale and Wally the Whale are swimming along side by side when they spot a whaling ship. Willy turns to Wally and says, "You know, I've lost a lot of family and friends to the whaling industry, and I'm in the mood for some revenge. What say we swim under that boat and blow water through our spouts? That'll be sure to capsize that vessel."

"That's a great idea," agrees Wally, and the two whales maneuver right beneath the ship, spout upwards with great force, and overturn the vessel, throwing all the crew into the sea.

"Hey, Wally! Now's our chance to really get revenge. What say we eat all those murdering sons of bitches!" shouts Willy rapaciously.

"No way," answers Wally. "I was all for the blow job, but I won't swallow seamen."

## Promises to Keep

Little Red Riding Hood's grandmother is lying in her bed when the wolf bursts through the door and stands above the bed panting.

"I'm going to tear you limb from limb!" growls the wolf.

"No, you won't," replies the grandmother, pulling out a revolver from under the covers. "You'll do as the story says and eat me!"

## Strange Pet

While out walking in the woods, a husband and wife discover an abandoned baby skunk. The wife takes an immediate liking to it, brings the little thing home, and makes it a pet. In fact, every night the skunk sleeps right between her legs.

What about the smell? Don't worry. The skunk's gotten quite used to it.

## Grin and Bear It

A prostitute accosts a koala bear and invites him to have sex with her. All night long the bear performs oral sex, much to her delight, given the animal's long ursine tongue. When all is done, the koala bounds out of the bed and heads for the door.

"Wait a minute!" protests the whore. "Aren't you going to pay me?"

"Pay you?" asks the bear incredulously.

Whipping out a dictionary, the woman opens to a page and points to the definition of *prostitute:* "One who performs sexual favors for money."

The bear flips the pages of the dictionary and points to the definition of *koala bear:* "Brown, furry creature who eats bushes and leaves."

## Logo Logic

Years ago, when the Exxon Corporation was called Esso, the company decided to use an animal as its logo. The ad people considered using a buzzing bee, but finally decided to use a tiger and the slogan "Put a Tiger in Your Tank." They felt that the company shouldn't be associated with an Esso bee.

## Wishful Thinking

Two men are out walking and come upon a dog licking its balls. "I wish I could do that," one of the men muses aloud.

The other man suggests, "Try patting it on the head, and maybe it'll let you."

## A Fish Story

In a Florida seaquarium marine biologists import a pair of dolphins in order to study their mating habits. The researchers soon discover that the dolphins can be provoked into a frenzy of sexual activity if they are fed a steady diet of baby seagulls and mynah birds.

Unfortunately, patrons of the seaquarium, especially youngsters, begin flocking to the dolphins' tank to watch them fornicate, thus creating a public nuisance and interfering with the biologists' research. To solve the problem, officials install a moat around the cage and place three ferocious lions, donated by the state of Florida, there to prevent people from coming up to the cage to watch the dolphins frolic.

One man, who had become rather addicted to watching the lusty loving of the dolphins, stuffs a cache of baby gulls and mynah birds into a sack and rigs a vine from the aquarium ceiling. Then he swings across the moat while the lions are asleep, feeds the birds to the dolphins, and gleefully watches them fornicate.

He is caught and arrested not for trespassing, but for a much more serious crime. He is thrown in the clink for transporting young gulls and mynahs over state lions for immoral porpoises.

## Last Ditch Effort

It's Operation Iraqi Freedom, and one of the donkeys used to carry supplies keels over, dies, and starts to swell up and stink. Three GIs are assigned the job of burying the beast, and right in the middle of the digging, Barbara Walters comes by with a news crew for an interview.

"What are you digging there, men," she asks, "a foxhole?"

"That's what it is! Absolutely!" they all shout.

## And the Winner Is . . .

A medieval king announces a quest. To the knight who returns within one week with the greatest number of Ping-Pong balls will go half the royal treasury and the hand in marriage of his daughter, the beautiful princess.

Many knights ride off, and one week later one comes back with a huge basket of Ping-Pong balls. He empties the basket, and out bounce a thousand balls.

A second knight presents two baskets heaped with two thousand balls.

Just before the king declares the second knight the winner, a third knight staggers into the castle. He's all scratched up and profusely bleeding, and on his back he carries a bulging and bloody sack.

"How many Ping-Pong balls do you have in that horrible-looking sack?" asks the king.

"Ping-Pong balls?" screams the man. "Shit! I thought you said, 'King Kong's balls!'"

### Hole-y Mole-y

A mama mole, a papa mole, and a baby mole all live in a little mole hole. One day the papa mole sticks his head out of the hole, sniffs the air, and says, "Yum! I smell maple syrup!"

The mama mole sticks her head out of the hole, sniffs the air and says, "Yum! I smell honey!"

The baby mole tries to stick his head out of the hole to sniff the air, but can't because the bigger moles are in the way, so he says, "Geez, all I can smell is molasses."

### Lord of the Flies

A happy little fly is buzzing around a barn when she happens upon a large pile of fresh cow manure. Feeling hungry, she flies to the irresistible delicacy and begins to pig out. She eats and eats and eats and eats some more. Finally, she decides she's had plenty. She washes her face with her tiny front legs, belches a few times, then attempts to fly away. But, alas, she's eaten far too much and can't get off the ground. Wondering what to do about this unpleasant situation, she looks around and spots a pitchfork leaning upright against the barn wall.

She realizes if she can just climb up that handle and jump off to become airborne, she'll be able to fly again. So, painstakingly she climbs to the top of the handle, takes a deep breath, spreads her tiny wings, and leaps off confidently. But she drops like a rock and splatters all over the floor. Dead Fly.

*Moral:* Never fly off the handle when you know you're full of shit.

## Animal Quickies

- Do you know that King Kong plays Ping-Pong with his ding-dong?

- If a man goes to bed with two women, how many animals will be in that bed?
  *A dozen: three asses, six calves, two pussies, and one dead cock.*

- Why don't chickens wear underwear?
  *You wouldn't either if your pecker was on your face.*

- What's gray and comes in gallons?
  *Elephants.*

- Why does an elephant have four feet?.
  *Because it would look silly with only six inches.*

- Where is an elephant's sex organ?
  *In his feet. If he steps on you, you're fucked.*

- What do you get when you cross an elephant with a prostitute?
  *A four-thousand-pound lay that does it for peanuts and will never forget you.*

- What do you get when you cross an elephant with a rhinoceros?
  *Elephino.*

- What do you get when you cross a donkey with an owl?
  *A smart ass that knows it all.*

- How many mice does it take to screw in a lightbulb?
  *Two, if the mice are very small.*

How many mice does it take to screw in a lightbulb?

- How do you circumcise a whale?
  *Use four skin divers.*

- Ninety percent of men who try Camels prefer women.

- The ideal man is like a beluga whale. He has a four-foot tongue and can breathe out of a hole in the top of his head.

- A man earned his living circumcising elephants. He hated the work, but the tips were big.

- What do the reindeers' wives do on Christmas night?
  *They go down to the Elks Club and blow a few bucks*

- What's the difference between beer nuts and deer nuts?
  *Beer nuts cost a buck fifty-nine. Deer nuts are under a buck.*

- What can a swan do that a duck can't and a lawyer should?
  *Stick its bill up its ass.*

- What do you call an adolescent rabbit?
  *A pubic hare.*

- What do you call a herd of masturbating bulls?
  *Beef strokin' off.*

- What's white and four feet long?
  *Moby's dick.*

- Where do you get virgin wool?
  *From ugly sheep.*

- What did Miss Piggy say to the muppet?
  *"I can't talk now. I've got a frog in my throat."*

- What's green and smells like Miss Piggy?
  *Kermit the Frog's face.*

- Why does Miss Piggy use a honey and vinegar douche?
  *Because Kermit likes sweet and sour pork.*

- What's the best way to eat a frog?
  *Place a little leg over each ear.*

- What sound does a horny toad make?
  *"Rub-it! Rub-it!"*

- What do you get when you cross a rooster and an owl?
  *A cock that stays up all night.*

- What do you get when you cross a rooster with an M&M?
  *A cock that melts in your mouth, not on your hand.*

- What do you get when you cross a donkey with an onion?
  *A piece of ass that brings tears to your eyes.*

- What do you call it when you cross a grouse and an owl?
  *A growl.*

- What do you call it when you cross a crow with a raven?
  *A craven.*

- What do you call it when you cross a falcon and a duck?
  *A dalcon.*

- Why is a sea lion like Tupperware?
  *They both work best with tight seals.*

- How do you tell the difference between boy sardines and girl sardines?
  *Look and see which can they come out of.*

- If the hawk is associated with war, the dove with peace, and the stork with the delivery of babies, what bird is associated with birth control?
  *The swallow.*

- What do you have if you have a mothball in one hand and a mothball in the other hand?
  *One hell of a moth.*

- How does a bartender know which men like Moosehead?
  *He looks for the ones with the antler scratches on their hips.*

- How does a woman get herself a mink?
  *The same way minks do.*

- What article of clothing does a bull enjoy most?
  *A tight Jersey.*

- What do large-mouthed fish make when they poop?
  *Bass turds.*

- Isn't it curious that in this world of ours there are more horses' asses than there are horses?

- I'm going to the giraffe party. It's mostly neck and a little tail.

- A couple bought a new kitten and named it Paderewski because it was the pianist.

- Big cats can be dangerous, but a little pussy never hurt anybody.

- The earthworm is a hermaphrodite that comes equipped with both male and female sex organs. Now there's a creature who really can go fuck itself.

- Whoever first said that "a dog is man's best friend" had never seen a pussy before.

- What is the similarity between a rattlesnake and a limp dick?
  *You don't screw with either one.*

- What's the biggest drawback of the jungle?
  *An elephant's foreskin.*

- Why did the guy call his dog Herpes?
  *Because he wouldn't heel.*

- If a sheep is a ram and a mule is an ass, how come a ram in the ass is a goose?

- How do you piss off Winnie the Pooh?
  *By sticking your finger in his honey.*

- The strangest story in the Bible is when it says that Abraham tied his ass to a tree and walked a mile.

- Have you heard that they've started castrating all the male horses in the former Soviet Union? It's just one more example of destallionization.

- FIRST MOUSE: "Are you a legmouse?"
  SECOND MOUSE: "No, I'm a titmouse."

- Save a tree; eat a beaver.

- Stop masturbating: A bird in the hand seldom gets into the bush.

## A Closing Yolk

If you think your life is bad, just think how bad the life of an egg is:

You only get laid once.

You only get eaten once.

They've got to boil you to get you hard.

It takes only two minutes to get soft.

You have to share a box with eleven other guys.

And the only chick who ever sat on your face was your mother!

Now don't you feel better?

# Vice
# Verse

Believe it or not (and I'll bet you don't), there exists an annual National Dirty Poetry Contest.

An aspiring creative writer from Connecticut works for a full year on his submission and eventually fashions what he believes to be the foulest and filthiest, rudest and raunchiest, sexiest and steamiest piece of verse ever concocted. With great confidence he sends it off to the National Dirty Poetry Contest, certain that he'll win the trophy—and I'll leave it to you to imagine what that looks like.

A month later he receives a plain brown envelope in the mail and inside finds an announcement typed on National Dirty Poetry Contest letterhead: "Congratulations. You have won second prize in the National Dirty Poetry Contest."

Stunned and depressed, the contestant calls NDPC headquarters and gets the judge on the line. "Sir," he complains, "I sent you what I felt to be the most foul and filthy, rude and raunchy, sexy and steamy poem I could imagine. Why did I only get second prize?"

"I understand your concern," sympathizes the judge. "Your poem was indeed the filthiest and foulest, rudest and raunchiest, sexiest and steamiest poem I had ever received for the competition. You are to be congratulated in crafting a poem that appeals totally to prurient interest and is devoid of any redeeming social value whatsoever.

"I was all set to award you the first-prize trophy when we received an entry from a graduate student out in Oregon. Incredibly, his poem was so foul and filthy, rude and raunchy, sexy and steamy—so appealing to prurient interest and so completely devoid of redeeming social value—that it made yours look like a nursery rhyme. So we awarded it first prize."

"Gee," sighs the Connecticut man, "I wonder if you could do me a favor. I'd like to learn from that poem. Would you read it to me over the telephone?"

"Are you kidding!" shouts the judge. "The FBI taps into my line. If I read the poem, they'd record it, and I'd be thrown into jail for life!"

"OK," replies the frustrated entrant. "Could you send it to me?"

"What!" screams the judge even more shrilly. "The feds often open my letters. If I send a piece like that through the mail, I could be thrown in jail for two lifetimes!"

"Well, then, could you read the poem to me on the phone and leave out the really dirty words?"

"If that's what you want, I'll do it," sighs the judge.

"Here it is:

Da da, da da, da da, da, da,
    Da da, da da, da da.
Da da, da da, da da, da da,
    Da da, da da, da da.

Da da, da da, da da, da da,
    Da da, da da, da da.
Da da, da da, da da, da da,
    Da da, da da, da fuck."

Just kidding, of course. There isn't really any National Dirty Poetry Contest, but there's a lot of national dirty poetry around that many of us share. Maybe I had a misspent childhood, but, when I was a little boy and dinosaurs roamed the earth, my gang and I sang songs about beans:

Beans, beans, good for the heart—
    The more you eat the more you fart.
The more you fart, the better you feel,
    So eat more beans at every meal.

And:

First marine, he found the bean, *parlez vous.*
Second marine, he cooked the bean, *parlez vous.*
    Third marine, he ate the bean
    And crapped all over the submarine—
    Inky dinky *parlez vous.*

We kids growing up in West Philadelphia also had great lascivious fun chanting an infernal array of devilish ditties. It was our first experience with aural sex:

## Asshole

Asshole, asshole,
    Asshole-dier went to war
To piss, to piss,
    To piss-tols at his side.
Fuck you, fuck you,
    Fuck you-riosity—
To fight for his cunt, to fight for his cunt,
    To fight for his cunt-te-ree.

## A Juvenile Classic

Miss Lucy had a steamboat.
    The steamboat had a bell.
Miss Lucy went to heaven.
    The steamboat went to

Hello, operator,
    Give me number nine,
And if you disconnect me,
    I'll chop off your

Behind the 'frigerator
    There was a piece of glass.
Miss Lucy sat upon it
    And it went straight up her

Ask me no more questions.
    I'll tell you no more lies.
The boys are in the girls room
    Zipping up their

Flies are in the city.
    Bees are in the town.
Miss Lucy and her boyfriend
    Are going all around

In the d-a-r-k,
    D-a-r-k, d-a-r-k,
Dark, dark, dark.


Miss Lucy had a baby.
    His name was Tiny Tim.
She put him in the bathtub
    To see if he could swim.


He swam to the bottom.
    He swam to the top.
Miss Lucy got excited
    And pulled him by the


Cocktail, ginger ale,
    Five cents a glass.
If you do not like it,
    You can stick it up your


Ask me no questions,
    And I'll tell you no lies.
A man got hit with a bucket of shit
    Right between the eyes.


## Having a Ball

Do your balls hang low?
    Can you swing them to and fro?
Can you tie them in a knot?
    Can you tie them in a bow?
Can you throw them o'er your shoulder
    Like a continental soldier?
Do your balls hang low?
    [This song is easily adapted to tits.]

### Hail, Columbus

In fourteen hundred ninety-two,
    Columbus sailed the ocean blue.
The ship hit a rock, he broke his cock,
    And pissed all over the crew.

### Fight Song

Alakazoo, alakazam,
    Son of a bitch, goddam,
Highty tighty, Christ almighty,
    Rah, rah, shit!

### Midnight Runs

Listen, my children, and you shall hear
The midnight ride of diarrhea:
Off with the covers, and on to the floor—
A fifty-foot dash to the bathroom door.
"Hasten, Jason, bring the basin!"
Plip-plop. Too late. Bring the mop.

### Frankly Speaking

Sally is a friend of mine.
    She resembles Frankenstein.
For a nickel or a dime
    She would do it any time.

### A Snow-White Song

Heigh-ho, heigh-ho!
It's off to the burlesque show.
    We pay two bits
    To see their tits.
Heigh-ho, heigh-ho!

Heigh-ho, heigh-ho!
It's off to the burlesque show.
We pay a buck
To see them fuck.
Heigh-ho, heigh-ho!

## Deflowered

You wore a tulip, a bright yellow tulip,
And I wore my BVDs.
First I caressed you, and then I undressed you.
Oh, what a sight to see.

I played with your titties, your white little titties,
Then down where the short hair grows.
You wore a tulip, a bright yellow tulip,
And I wore a big red rose.

## Deflowered Again

Rose's are red.
Violet's are blue.
They wore see through bras.
That's how I knew.

## Tah-Rah-Rah-Boom-Dee-Ay

Tah-rah-rah-boom-dee-ay
How did you get that way?
It was the boy next door.
He threw me on the floor.

He lifted up my skirt
And told me, "This won't hurt."
He stuck his thingy in.
Said, "This won't be a sin."

My mother was surprised
To see my belly rise.
My father jumped for joy.
It was a baby boy.

### Two Mid Evil Verses

In days of old, when knights were bold,
And paper wasn't invented,
They wiped their ass with tufts of grass,
And they were quite contented.

In days of old, when knights were bold,
And women weren't particular,
They lined them all against the wall
And fucked them perpendicular.

### On a Roll

Now this is Number One—
And the fun has just begun!
Roll me over, lay me down, and do it again.

Now this is Number Two—
Please accept my thanks to you.
Roll me over, lay me down, and do it again.

CHORUS
*Roll me over in the clover;*
*Roll me over, lay me down, and do it again.*

Now this is Number Three—
And I'm fucking fancy free!
Roll me over, lay me down, and do it again.

Now this is Number Four—
I know what my pussy's for!
Roll me over, lay me down, and do it again.

Now this is Number Five—
Are you really still alive?
Roll me over, lay me down, and do it again,

Now this is Number Six—
And I'm getting plenty kicks.
Roll me over, lay me down, and do it again.

Now this is Number Seven—
And for me it's just pure heaven!
Roll me over, lay me down, and do it again.

Now this is Number Eight—
And the bastard's just dead weight!
Roll me over, lay me down, and do it again.

Now this is Number Nine—
And you're dong is in just fine!
Roll me over, lay me down, and do it again.

Now this is Number Ten—
And I've worn out four big men!
Roll me over, lay me down, and do it again.

### Spellbound

'Twas love at first sight
For Ephraim and Kay.
Now when you see happy
Eph, you see Kay.

Rhyme and meter play an important role in dirty humor, as witness these passages of pornographic poetry:

### Bees Do It

This is the story of the bee
Whose sex is very hard to see.
You cannot tell a he from she,
But he can tell, and so can she.

The little bee is never still,
So has no time to take the pill—
And that is why in times like these
There are so many sons of bees.

### No Joking Matter

It's tough to find,
    For love or money,
A joke that's clean,
    And also funny.


### Such a Deal

She offered her honor.
    He honored her offer.
So all night long
    It was on her and off her.


### Turning Over a New Leaf

Here's to Eve,
    The mother of our race,
Who wore her leaves
    In the proper place.

Here's to Adam,
    The father of us all,
Who planted his root
    When the leaves began to fall.


### Madam, I'm Adam

I'll tell you a little story,
    Just a story I have heard,
And you'll swear it's all a fable,
    But it's gospel, every word.

When the Lord made father Adam,
    They say He laughed and sang,
And sewed him up the belly
    With a little piece of whang.

But when the Lord was finished,
    He found He'd measured wrong;
For when the whang was knotted,
    'Twas several inches long.

Said He, " 'Tis but eight inches,
    So I guess I'll let it hang."
So He left on Adam's belly,
    That little piece of whang.

But when the Lord made mother Eve,
    I imagine He did snort,
When He found the whang he sewed her with
    Was several inches short.

" 'Twill leave an awful gap," said He,
    "But I should give a damn.
She can fight it out with Adam
    For that little piece of whang."

So ever since that fateful day
    When human life began,
There's been a constant struggle
    'Twixt the woman and the man.

## Three Mary Ditties

Mary had a little sheep,
    And with the sheep she went to sleep.
The sheep turned out to be a ram.
    Now Mary has a little lamb.

Mary had a little lamb.
    She also had a bear.
You always see her little lamb,
    But you never see her bare.

And with the sheep she went to sleep.

Mary had a little plane.
  In it she loved to frisk.
Wasn't she a silly girl
  Her little *?

## Birth Control
There was an old woman
Who lived in a shoe.
She didn't have any children—
SHE knew what to do!

## A Miss Is as Good
Little Miss Muffet sat on a tuffet
  Eating a Kurd all day.
Along came a spider, who sat down beside her,
  And with her he had his whey.

## Bathroom Humor
Tom, Tom, the bathroom man:
  He's the keeper of the company can.
He picks up the papers,
  And he rolls up the towels,
And he listens to the music
  Of the discontented bowels.

## Gone with the Wind
A burp is just a breath of air
  That cometh from the heart.
But when it takes the lower route,
  It cometh out a fart.

## The Lesser of Two Evils
Better to fart and bear the shame
Than not to fart and bear the pain.

### The Bad Boy
Little Johnny with a grin
    Drank up all of Pappy's gin.
Mother said, when he got plastered,
    "Go to bed, you little love child."

### How to Make It
To please 'em,
Don't tease 'em.
Just seize 'em
And squeeze 'em.

### On Vibrators
The thought occurs
That one good dude is worth
A thousand whirrs.

## And Tyler Too
Two men had a contest to see which of them could use the word *Timbuktu* more cleverly in a poem.
The first wrote this verse:

While passing through a foreign land,
    We gazed across the burning sand.
A caravan came into view.
    Its destination: Timbuktu.

The second man topped the first with this approach:

Tim and I on safari went.
    We spied three maidens in a tent.
They were three, and we were two,
    So I bucked one and Tim bucked two.

## Titty Ditty

A flat-chested woman goes to a Dr. Jugski to have her breasts enlarged. The doctor tells her to close her eyes each day and call up images of herself with big boobs. At the same time she is to recite a little rhyme. Several days after her visit, she's sitting on a bus with her eyes closed, concentrating hard, and saying the poem that the doctor ordered:

> Mary had a little lamb.
> It loved her just to bits.
> I close my eyes and fantasize
> That I shall have big tits.

A man sitting next to her asks, "Excuse me, madam, but are you a patient of Dr. Jugski?"

"Yes, I am," the woman says with great astonishment. "How could you possibly know that?"

The man closes his eyes, thinks hard, and recites,

> "Hickory dickory dock . . ."

## The Root of the Problem

There was a man named Slippery Dick
  Who was cursed from birth with a corkscrew prick.
He spent his life on a fruitless hunt
  Seeking a girl with a spiral cunt.
One day he found her and near dropped dead
  'Cause the goddam thing had a left-hand thread!

## Quite a Führer

Hitler had only just one ball.
  Göring had two, but very small.
Himmler had something similar,
  And poor old Goebbels had no balls at all.

—song popular among American troops in World War II

## Egyptian Conniptions

The sexual urge of the camel
Is greater than anyone thinks.
In moments of amorous passion,
He even consorts with the Sphinx.

But the Sphinx's posterior passage
Has been clogged by the sands of the Nile,
Which accounts for the hump on the camel—
And the Sphinx's inscrutable smile.

## Lap of Luxury

'Twas the night before Christmas,
    When all through the house,
Not a creature was stirring,
    Not even a mouse.

Mom was carrying toys
    In her see-through nightgown,
Showing her person
    From her middle on down.

When she crept past the crib
    Of her little boy,
Her youngest and sweetest,
    Her pride and her joy.

His eyes opened wide
    As he stared from his cot
And saw everything
    Including Mom's twat.

He didn't even notice
    The toys on her lap.
He just asked her, "For who
    Is that little fur cap?"

His mother said, "Hush,"
    And she laughed with delight.
"I think I'll give that
    To your father tonight!"

### A Visit from St. Prickless

'Twas the night before Christmas,
    And all through the house,
Every creature felt shitty,
    Even the mouse.

With Mom at the whorehouse
    And Dad smoking grass,
I'd just settled down
    To a nice piece of ass.

When out on the lawn
    I heard such a clatter,
I sprang from my piece
    To see what was the matter.

Then out on the lawn
    I saw a man prickless.
I knew in a moment
    It must be St. Nicholas.

He came down the chimney
    Like a bat out of hell.
I knew in a moment
    The fucker had fell.

With pretzels and beer
    He filled up the stocking
And a big rubber dick
    For my sister for cocking.

He rose up the chimney
    With a thunderous fart.
The son of a bitch
    Blew the chimney apart.

He swore and he cussed
    As he rose out of sight,
"Fuck you, and fuck you,
    And all have a good night."

### An Epitaph

Here lie the bones of Martha Jones.
For her Hell has no terrors.
Born a virgin—died a virgin:
No hits, no runs, no errors.

### Sprightly Suzanne

Suzanne was a girl
    With plenty of class
Who knocked 'em all dead
    When she wiggled her

Eyes at the boys
    As girls sometimes do,
To make it quite plain
    That she wanted to

Take in a movie
    Or go for a sail
Or hurry on home
    For a nice piece of

Cake, with some ice cream,
    Or a slice of roast duck,
For after each meal
    She was ready to

Go for a ride
　　Or a stroll with some hick
Or with any young man
　　With a sizeable

Roll of big bills
　　And a pretty good front,
And if he talked right,
　　She would show him her

Little pet dog,
　　Who was subject to fits,
And maybe she'd let him
　　Take hold of her

Little white hand
　　Or hug her real quick,
And with a sly smile
　　She would tickle his

Chin while she showed him
　　A trick learned in France
And would ask the young fellow
　　To take off his

Coat, while she sang
　　Of the sweet Swanee shore,
For, whatever she was,
　　Suzanne was no bore!

Even dirty prose can rely on rhyme and meter:

## Older Is Better

Among the many reasons why older women are the best lovers is that they don't smell, they don't yell, they don't tell, they don't swell—and they're grateful as hell!

## The Creation of a Pussy

Seven wise men with knowledge so fine
    Created a pussy to their design.
First was a butcher, smart with a wit.
    Using a knife, he gave it a slit.
Second was a carpenter, strong and bold.
    With a hammer and chisel he gave it a hole.
Third was a tailor, tall and thin.
    Using red velvet, he lined it within.
Fourth was a hunter, short and stout.
    With a piece of fox fur he lined it without.
Fifth was a fisherman, nasty as hell.
    Threw in a fish and gave it a smell.
Sixth was a preacher whose name was McGhee.
    Touched it and blessed it and said it could pee.
Last came a sailor, a dirty little runt.
    He sucked it and fucked it and called it a cunt.

## The Ins and Outs

Man on top of woman
    Hasn't long to stay,
His head is full of nonsense,
    His ass is full of play.

He goes in like a lion,
    He comes out like a lamb,
And when he buttons up his pants,
    He isn't worth a damn.

## Shortchanged

A man pays a nickel to enter a pay-toilet booth. Later he's found dead, sitting on the toilet seat with a bullet through his head and this note around his neck:

"Here I sit, brokenhearted.
Paid a nickel, and only farted."

## What's in a Name?

A father is sitting at home with his four daughters when there's a knock on the door. A young man appears and announces:

> "My name is Lance,
>> And I'd like the chance
> To go to the dance
>> With your daughter Nance."

Soon after Lance and Nance have left, another guy shows up and says,

> "My name is Joe,
>> And I'd like to go
> To the picture show
>> With your daughter Flo."

Then along comes yet another fellow who announces:

> "My name is Teddy,
>> And I'm all ready
> To eat some spaghetti
>> With your daughter Betty."

Off go Teddy and Betty. About an hour later there's a frightfully loud knocking. The father opens the door and in staggers an obviously drunk fellow, who begins to slur:

> "My name is Tucker . . ."

## Just Ducky

A handsome young farmer goes to a whorehouse and offers a prostitute a duck in exchange for her favors. She agrees and so enjoys his whoopie that she says she'll give him back the duck for one more session.

As the fellow is walking home, the duck flies out of his hand and is hit by a passing produce truck. The truck driver feels sorry for the young man and gives him a dollar.

When the farmer gets home, his father asks him how his day has been.

The son says, "I got a fuck for a duck, a duck for a fuck, and a buck for a fucked-up duck."

## Not Calling a Spade a Spade

What's another name for a successful proctologist? *A super-duper pooper snooper.*

## New Math

The heat of the meat + the mass of the ass = the angle of the dangle.

## Passing Fancy

Men make passes at girls who drain glasses.

## Graffiti

If you sprinkle when you tinkle, be a sweetie and wipe the seatie.

## The Fall of Rome

During the burning of Rome, the emperor Nero engaged in a wild sex orgy, frequently stopping to urinate. You could say that Nero diddled, piddled, and fiddled while Rome burned.

# A Leer of Limericks

The limerick packs laughs anatomical
Into space that is quite economical.
    But the good ones I've seen
    So seldom are clean,
And the clean ones so seldom are comical.
              *—Vyvyan Holland*

It needn't have ribaldry's taint
Or strive to make everyone faint.
    There's a type that's demure
    And perfectly pure,
Though it helps quite a lot if it ain't.
              *—Don Marquis*

Let us celebrate the limerick, a highly disciplined exercise in verse that is the major fixed poetic form indigenous to the English language. While other forms of poetry, such as the sonnet and ode, are borrowed from other countries, the limerick is an original English creation and the most quoted of all poetic patterns in our language.

Although the limerick is named for a county in Ireland, it was not created there. One theory says that Irish mercenaries used to compose verses in limerick form to each other and then join in a chorus of "When we get back to Limerick town, 'twill be a glorious morning":

> The limerick's start is obscure,
> Especially forms that are pure.
> But this wins all bets:
> The older it gets,
> It gets bluer and bluer and bluer.

> The limerick's form is complex.
> Its contents run chiefly to sex.
> It burgeons with virgins
> And prurient urgings
> And drips with erotic effects.

It was the English writer Edward Lear who, in his *Book of Nonsense* (1846), gave the form its name and its lightheartedness. Lear penned his five-line ditties for children, but the limerick soon bounded out of the nursery and into the marketplace, pubs, and campuses. As Donald Chain Black quips, "All good limericks have dirty faces":

> The limerick is furtive and mean.
> You must keep her in close quarantine.
> Or she sneaks to the slums
> And promptly becomes
> Disorderly, drunk, and obscene.
> —Morris Bishop

It has been estimated that between ten thousand and a million limericks—good, mediocre, and indelicate—have been published. Some critics go out on a limerick and maintain that there are only two kinds—the clean ones and the funny ones. Here are my favorite funny ones:

## Monopoly

In the Garden of Eden lay Adam,
Complacently stroking his madam,
    And loud was his mirth,
    For on all of the earth
There were only two balls—and he had 'em.

## Gang Bang

There was a young lady named Gloria,
Who was had by Sir Gerald Du Maurier,
    And then by six men,
    Sir Gerald again,
And the band at the Waldorf Astoria.

## Grave Humor

There was a young man named McBride,
Who fell in a shithouse and died.
    His heartbroken brother
    Fell into another,
And now they're interred side by side.

## Unkindest Cut

There was a young pirate named Gates,
Who did the fandango on skates.
    He fell on his cutlass,
    Which rendered him nutless,
And practically useless on dates.

### Great Buns

There once was a comely Creole,
Whose humor was markedly droll.
At a masquerade ball,
Dressed in nothing at all,
She backed in as a Parker House roll.

### Rhythm Method

A fellow who wasn't an amateur
Had an organ quite large in diameter,
But it wasn't the size
That brought tears to maids' eyes:
'Twas the rhythm—iambic pentameter.

### Aerial Act

A fellow from cushy Bel Air
Was fucking a girl·on the stair.
The bannister broke,
But he doubled his stroke—
And finished her off in midair.

### Music to Our Rears

There was a young fellow from Sparta,
A really magnificent farter.
On the strength of one bean
He'd fart "God Save the Queen"
And Beethoven's "Moonlight Sonata."

### Sticking It Out

There was a young fellow named Lancelot,
Whom his neighbors all looked on askance a lot.
For whenever he'd pass
A presentable lass,
The front of his pants would advance a lot.

### In the Spirit

There was a young man from the Coast
Who had an affair with a ghost.
 At the height of orgasm
 Said the pallid phantasm,
"I think I can feel it—almost!"

### Around the Bend

There was a young fellow named Kent,
Whose dick was so long that it bent.
 To save himself trouble,
 He stuck it in double—
And, instead of coming, he went.

### Three's Company

There was a young fellow from Lyme
Who lived with three wives at a time.
 When asked, "Why the third?"
 He said, "One's absurd,
And bigamy, sir, is a crime!"

### Fireworks

Nymphomaniacal Alice
Used dynamite sticks for a phallus.
 They found her vagina
 In North Carolina,
And bits of her tits down in Dallas.

### For the Dirty-Minded

There was a young lass from Madras
Who had a magnificent ass—
 Not rounded and pink,
 As you probably think:
It was gray, had long ears, and ate grass.

There was a young lass from Madras. . . .

### Which Comes First?
There once was a man from Montmartre
Who puzzled for months over Sartre:
   "If it's true that *essence*
   Precedes *existence*,
I must first be before I can fartre."

### It's Such a Little Thing
There was a young man from Berlin
Whose tool was the size of a pin.
   Said his girl with a laugh,
   As she fondled his staff,
"Well, this won't be much of a sin."

### It's a Business Doing Pleasure
A notorious harlot named Hearst
In the pleasures of men is well versed,
   Reads the sign o'er the head
   Of her well-rumpled bed,
"The Customer Always Comes First."

### The Bermuda Triangle
I wooed a stewed nude in Bermuda.
I was rude, but by God!, she was lewder.
   It was crude she was wooed
   In the nude by a dude.
I pursued her, subdued her, and screwed her!

### Monkey Business
There was a young tar from the sea
Who screwed a baboon in a tree.
   The results were most horrid—
   All ass and no forehead,
Four balls, and a purple goatee.

### The Men Who Came at Dinner
There was a young fellow named Skinner
Who took a young lady to dinner.
    At a quarter to nine
    They sat down to dine,
And at twenty to ten it was in her—
    The dinner, not Skinner—
Skinner was in her before dinner.

There was a young fellow named Tupper
Who took a young lady to supper.
    At a quarter to nine
    They sat down to dine,
And at twenty to ten it was up her.
    Not the supper—not Tupper—
It was some son of a bitch named Skinner!


No way can I compete with these masterpieces of merriment and meter. Still, I can't resist trying some of my own, pale reflections though they may be:


### My Turn
I'll now make a limerick that's betterer,
Or my name isn't Richard H. Lederer.
    You may think it odd o' me
    To write about sodomy,
Fellatio, fucking, et ceterer.


### The Unfetterer
An old cunning linguist, Rich Lederer,
Met a girl, and he wanted to get her. Her
    Hips were so dominant,
    Her bosoms so prominent,
That he had a strong urge to unsweater her.

## My Dirty Mind

I'm in need of some psychoanalysis.
For all I can think about callous is:
    Twats, asses, and tits,
    Piss, farts, semen, shits,
Lips, tips, nipples, scrotums, and phalluses.

## Australia Genitalia

An incredible beast is the kangaroo—
Gives his mate a marsupial bangaroo.
    She spreads legs asunder.
    He enters Down Under
With his firm, aboriginal whangaroo.

## The Truth About Sigmund

Doctor Freud, who was quite paraneud,
With his sex organ constantly teud.
    Mrs. Freud was anneud
    And not overjeud
That Freud wasn't filling her veud.

## Ramming It Home

The shepherd, to ward off the blues,
Tries flocking, and sheepishly screws.
    "Are the stars out tonight?"
    He sings in his plight,
"I only have eyes for ewes."

## The Right Tool

A fuckstress from north Alabama
Complained to her swain when he'd wham her:
    "You've got such a fat ass."
    He replied to the lass,
"Can't drive a spike with a tack hammer!"

### Gorilla My Heart

All the ladies go ape for old King Kong
And his hairy and humongous ding-dong.
    He's tall and dark and
    Has girls right in his hand.
With his balls they all like to play Ping-Pong.

### Fish Story

A maiden who lived on Cape Cod
And was blessed with a beautiful bod,
    Met an old master baiter,
    Who, wishing to sate her,
Fucked her hook, line, and sinker and rod.

### Stutter Nonsense

Said a stammering fellow named Stu,
"Sh-sh-shove it up your g-gazoo!
    Eat sh-sh-sh-shit!
    Suck t-t-t-tit!
And f-f-f-f-f-fuck you!"

### Warmest Regards

You loved me, then left me alone
To rot here, to moan, and to groan.
    Well, I'm not one to judge,
    And I don't hold a grudge,
But please throw your mother a bone!

### Inner Space

A corpulent girl from Ignatius
Had a cunt that was wonderfully spacious.
    Inside could be found
    A fish and a hound,
A gorilla, a whale, and—good gracious!

## Musical Shares
A flautist from Norwalk, Connecticut,
Let her colleagues get under her petticoat.
   The brass section fucked her,
   As did the conductor—
A breach of professional etiquette.

## Barnyard Language
A tired old hen lived in Worcester,
Who didn't lay eggs like she uorcester.
   As a big morale borcester,
   They brought in a rorcester
Who gorcester, sedorcester, and jorcester.

## Two Abbreviated Limericks
When an amorous Mr. first Kr.,
On her lips he encountered a Blr.
   Since she couldn't be Mrs.,
   He refocused his Krs.
At her Sr., which thoroughly Pr.


The president of a big co.
Once threatened to fire and to do.
   Cute secretary
   Who wouldn't make merry.
So they quit, and he never did ho.

# Jumping to Confusions

### The Italian Who Went to Detroit

Onea day Ima go to Detroit to a bigga hotel. Inna morning I go down to eat somea breakfast. I tella the waitress I wanna two piss toast. She bringa me only onea piss. I tella her I wanna two piss. She say go to the toilet. I say, you no understand: I wanna two piss on my plate.

She say you better no piss on the plate, you sonna ma beach. I donna even know the lady ana she calla me sonna ma beach.

Later I go to eat somea lunch at a bigga restaurant. The waitress she bringa me a spoon ana knife, but no fock. I tella her I wanna fock. She tella me everybody wanna fock. I tella her, you no understand, I wanna fock on the table. She say you better notta fock on the table, you sonna ma beach. I don't even know this lady, ana she calla me a sonna ma beach.

So I go back to my room inna hotel, ana there's no shit on my bed. I call the manager ana tella him I wanna shit. He tella to go to the toilet. So I say you no understand, I wanna shit onna bed.

He say, you better no shit on the bed, you sonna ma beach. I don't even know the man ana he calla me sonna ma beach.

I go to check out, ana the man at the desk, he say, peace to you. I say, piss onna you, too, you sonna ma beach.

Then I go back to Italy!

### Best Joke, Bar None

It's a hot day in Minnesota. Helga has hung the wash out to dry, put a roast in the oven, then gone downstairs to pick up some dry cleaning.

"Gootness, it's hot," she muses to herself as she walks down Main Street. She passes by a tavern and thinks, "Vy nodt?" so she walks in and takes a seat at the bar. The bartender comes up and asks her what she would like to drink. "Ya know," Helga says, "it is so hot I tink I'll have myself a cold beer."

The bartender asks, "Anheuser Busch?"

Helga blushes and replies, "Vell fine, tanks, and how's yer pecker?"

### Funny Money

A Chinese lady on holiday in London goes to a bank to change some Hong Kong dollars into pounds. She asks what the exchange rate is, and the teller says, "HK$12.50 for one British pound." She goes ahead and changes some money.

The next day she needs more pounds, so she goes back to the bank. This time the teller informs her, "HK$12.50 for one British pound." She goes ahead and changes some money.

The next day she needs more pounds, so she goes back to the bank. This time the teller informs her, "HK$12.80 for one British pound."

The Chinese lady complains, "What's going on? Yesterday it was only $12.50, and today it's $12.80?"

The teller explains, "Fluctuations."

"Well fuck you Caucasians, too!"

## The Wayside Chapel

An Englishwoman plans to visit Switzerland. She writes to a Swiss friend who recommends a particular place where she can stay, describing the apartment in profuse detail. Reading the friend's letter, the Englishwoman notes that the description contains nothing about a WC (water closet, or toilet). She writes back asking him the whereabouts of the WC.

The friend is a very poor student of English, so he asks the parish priest if he can help in the matter. Together they try to discover the meaning of the letters WC, and the only solution they can find is *Wayside Chapel*. The friend then writes the following note to the English lady:

*Dear Madam:*

*I take great pleasure in informing you that the WC is situated in the center of a beautiful grove of pine trees nine miles from the place you wish to stay.*

*It is capable of holding 220 people, with standing room for 50 more, and it is open on Sundays and Thursdays only. As a great number of people visit the WC during the summer months, I would suggest that you come early, although there is plenty of standing room. This is an unfortunate situation, particularly if you are in the habit of going regularly.*

*You will, no doubt, be glad to know that a good number bring their own lunch and make a day of it, while others, who can afford to go by car, arrive just in time. I would especially recommend that your ladyship go on Thursday, when there is an organ accompaniment. The acoustics are excellent, and the congregation can hear even the most delicate sounds. For the children, there is a special time and place so that they will not disturb the elders.*

*It may interest you to know that my daughter met her husband in the WC and it was there that they were married. I can remember the rush there was for seats. Two people had to sit in the space usually occupied by one. It was wonderful to see the expressions on their faces, faces flushed with pride.*

*The newest attractions are plush seats and a bell donated by a wealthy resident of the district. It rings every time a person enters. My wife is rather delicate, so she can't go regularly. Despite her great need, it has been a year since she last went. Naturally, it pains her very much not to go more often.*

*I shall be delighted to reserve the best seat for you, if you wish, where you will be seen by all.*

*Hoping to have been of some service to you,*

*I remain, sincerely,*
*Etienne*

## Field-Replaceable Mouse Balls

This text is said to have come out of an IBM ordering information catalog. The instructions refer to the rubber ball inside a computer mouse that guides the cursor on the monitor:

Mouse balls are now available as a field-replaceable unit. If a mouse fails to operate, or should perform erratically, it may be in need of a ball replacement. Because of the delicate nature of this procedure, replacement of mouse balls should be attempted only by trained personnel.

Before ordering, determine type of mouse balls required by examining the underside of the mouse. Domestic balls will be larger and harder than foreign balls. Ball removal procedures differ, depending upon manufacturer of the mouse.

Foreign balls can be replaced using the pop-off method and domestic balls replaced using the twist-off method. Mouse balls are not usually static sensitive. However, excessive handling can result in sudden discharge. Upon completion of ball replacement, the mouse may be used immediately.

It is recommended that each servicer have a pair of balls for maintaining optimum customer satisfaction, and that any customer missing his balls should suspect local personnel of removing these necessary functional items.

Everybody who has a dog calls him Rover or Spot.
I call mine Sex.

## What Not to Name Your Dog

Everybody who has a dog calls him Rover or Spot. I call mine Sex.

Sex has been very embarrassing to me. When I went to the City Hall to renew his dog license, I told the clerk that I would like to have a license for Sex.

He said, "I'd like to have one, too."

When I said, "But this is a dog," he said he didn't care what she looked like.

Then I said, "But you don't understand. I've had Sex since I was nine years old."

He said that I must have been quite a kid.

When I got married and went on my honeymoon, I took the dog with me. I told the motel clerk that I' wanted a room for my wife and me and a special room for Sex. He said that every room in the place was for sex. I said, "You don't understand. Sex keeps me awake at night."

"Me, too," said the clerk.

One day I entered Sex in a contest, but before the competition began, Sex ran away. Another contestant asked me why I was standing there looking around. I told her that I planned to have Sex in the competition. She told me that I should have sold my own tickets. "But you don't understand," I said. "I had hoped to have Sex on TV."

She called me a show-off.

When my wife and I separated, we went to court to fight for custody of the dog. I said, "Your Honor, I had Sex before I was married."

The judge said, "Me, too."

Then I told him that after I was married, Sex left me.

He said, "Me, too."

Last night Sex ran off again. I spent hours looking around town for him. A cop came up to me and asked, "What are you doing in this alley at four o'clock in the morning?"

"I'm looking for Sex," I said.

My case comes up next Friday.

## Accommodating Hostess

A New York woman throws a dinner party. One of the guests is a tall, handsome Texan. "Is there anything I can do for you?" she asks, fluttering her lashes.

"Yes, ma'am, I sure could use a piece of ass."

The hostess nods, takes the Texan into the bedroom, removes her clothes, and engages in a steamy session of lovemaking with him. When they are done, she again asks suggestively, "Now, handsome, is there anything else I can do for you?"

"Well, ma'am," he replies, "I still could use that piece of ass for my drink."

## Gusty and Lusty

An American GI is out sightseeing in London on a particularly windy day when he passes a trim little English miss. At that very moment a particularly zesty gust of wind blows her billowing skirt up over her head and exposes some of her choice and tender parts. The GI's eyes fairly pop, and he can't help but stare as she struggles to control her apparel. Being a bright young fellow, he decides to make a little conversation.

"It's a bit airy, isn't it?" he ventures solicitously.

" 'Ow observing of you," she snaps. "And 'ow would you 'ave it? Ostrich feathers?"

## From a Hole in the Ground

A preacher wanted to raise money for his church, and being told that there was a fortune to be made in horseracing, he decided to purchase one and enter him in the races. At the local auction, however, the going price for a horse was so steep that he ended up buying a donkey instead. The preacher decided that he might as well go ahead and enter it in the races, and to his surprise the donkey came in third. The next day the racing sheets carried this headline:

## PREACHER'S ASS SHOWS

The preacher was so pleased with the donkey that he entered it in another race, and this time it won. The headlines blared:

## PREACHER'S ASS OUT IN FRONT

The bishop was so upset with this kind of publicity that he ordered the preacher not to enter the donkey in another race. The newspaper printed this headline:

## BISHOP SCRATCHES PREACHER'S ASS

This was just too much for the bishop, and he ordered the preacher to get rid of the animal. The preacher decided to give it to a nun in a nearby convent. The headlines the next day announced:

## NUN HAS BEST ASS IN TOWN

The bishop fainted. He informed the nun that she would have to dispose of the donkey, and she finally found a farmer willing to buy it for ten dollars. The paper announced the transaction this way:

## NUN PEDDLES ASS FOR TEN BUCKS

They buried the bishop the next day.

## Get the L out of Here

A couple on a blind date visit a carnival that has been set up at a local park. They go for a ride on the merry-go-round, but she seems kind of bored. "What would you like to do now?" he asks.

"I wanna get weighed."

So he takes her over to the concession where there's a scale and a man who guesses your weight. He looks at the woman and says, "123 pounds," and he's absolutely correct.

Then they bomb around on the bumper cars, but she still looks bored. Again he asks her what she would like to do next, and again she whines, "I wanna get weighed." So he takes her back to the man at the scales, and, of course, the weight guesser hits her weight right on the nose.

She still looks bored, so he takes her for a ride on the roller coaster, but she still says, "I wanna get weighed."

"There's a screw loose here somewhere," he thinks, so he takes her back home even though it's only ten o'clock. At the door he leaves her with a perfunctory handshake.

The woman's mother asks her, "What's the matter, dear? You're home so early. Didn't you have a good time?"

"No," answers the woman, "I had a wousy time."

## Horse Sense

While hunting down some low-down murderous varmints, the Lone Ranger is captured. He manages to whisper a message into Silver's ear. The horse rears back, whinnies, and charges off to get help in a town many miles away.

The bad guys decide to take Loney out into the desert and tie him, naked, to a stake. Once they are satisfied that he is secured, they leave him to die slowly.

For two days, the Lone Ranger survives by sheer power of will. As the third dawn breaks, he hears the thundering of Silver's hooves. Up gallops the faithful horse with a naked redhead on his back.

"Shit, Silver," screams the masked man, "I said *posse!*"

## Impish Humor

During an evening of bending the elbow at a local watering hole, O'Malley asks the bartender, "Would you give me a free drink if I showed you the most amazing musical act you've ever seen?"

"Yes, I guess so," says the bartender.

O'Malley takes out an attaché case and pulls out a little man, just one foot high, and a tiny piano and stool. "Go ahead, Liam, tickle the ivories."

Tiny Liam leaps onto the piano stool and pounds out a medley of tunes to absolute perfection, his little fingers flying over the keys in a veritable blur.

"That is amazing!" shouts the bartender. "The drink is yours. Where did you ever find this fellow?"

"Well," says O'Malley. "Last month I was tramping through the bogs of Ireland, and one day I came upon one of the little folk, an old, half-deaf leprechaun who was so weak that I could barely hear his voice crying out for help. His miniature jacket was caught on a thornbush, and he was dangling and flailing about. Very carefully, lifted him off the thorn and set him down on the old sod.

"In a weak and wizened voice he thanked me for my efforts and offered to grant me one wish, any wish I requested. Well, I knew exactly what I wanted, and I made the wish. Unfortunately, he thought I asked him for a twelve-inch *pianist!*"

## Fits like a Glove

A young man wishes to buy his girlfriend a birthday gift. As they have not been dating very long, he decides that a pair of gloves will strike just the right note—romantic, but not too personal.

Unfortunately, the clerk assigned to wrapping the gift puts into the package a pair of panties that happened to be sitting right next to the gloves. When the girlfriend opens the package of panties, she reads this note:

*Darling: I chose these because I noticed that you are not in the habit of wearing any when we go out in the evening. I thought about buying you the long ones with buttons but decided on the short ones because they are so easy to remove. I bought you white ones because the lady I bought them from showed me a pair she had been wearing for three weeks and they were hardly soiled. I had her try yours on and she really looked smart.*

"*I wish I could be there to put them on you for the first time, as no doubt other hands will come in contact with them before I have a chance to see you in them. When you take them off, please remember to blow in them before putting them away as they will naturally be a little damp from wearing. I can hardly wait to see you in them. Please be sure to wear them for our upcoming date.*

# Diddles

Remember Oedipus? He was a complex Greek king who married a woman just like the girl that married dear old dad. He was a prince of a guy who married a woman old enough to be his mother—and that's just what she turned out to be.

Before he did that, Oedipus was challenged by a riddle put to him by the Sphinx: "What goes on four legs in the morning, on two at noon, and on three at night?" Oedipus, one of the first game-show contestants, answered the riddle correctly and thus became Oedipus Rex. His solution was "Man. In infancy he crawls, in his prime he walks, and in old age he leans on a staff."

Riddles are perhaps the most ancient of all verbal puzzles, dating back at least 2,500 years. Just as time-honored and challenging are diddles—riddles in which the question, answer, or both are on the randy side. As the following blue-two-liners illustrate, diddles, like riddles, have become part of the oral folklore that we share in common, and I do mean common:

- Three men are in a whorehouse. One is hurrying up the stairs to one of the rooms, another is leaving the establishment, and the third is getting it on with one of the women. What is the nationality of each man?
  *Russian, Finnish, and Himalayan.*

- How can you tell the clan of a Scotsman?
  *You lift up his kilt, and if you see a Quarter Pounder underneath, you know he's a McDonald.*

- If having your tonsils out is called a tonsillectomy and having your appendix out is called an appendectomy, what do you call a sex-change operation in which a woman becomes a man?
  *An addadictomy.*

- When a man has a sex change, what's the most painful part of the operation?
  *Having the salary cut in half.*

- What's better than roses on your piano?
  *Tulips on your organ.*

- What do breasts and electric trains have in common?
  *They're both designed for children, but Daddy gets to play with them.*

- Who was the first accountant in the Bible?
  *Adam. He turned over a leaf and made an entry.*

- Who was the first soft-drink bottler in the Bible?
  *Adam. He made Eve's cherry pop.*

- Where in the Bible do we read about the first computers?
  *In Genesis. Eve offered Adam an Apple and played with his Wang.*

- Who was the first carpenter in the Bible?
  *Eve. She made Adam's little peanut stand.*

- Who are the three most constipated men in the Bible?
  *Cain, because he wasn't Abel; Methuselah, who sat on the throne for nine hundred years; and Moses—God gave him two tablets and sent him into the wilderness.*

- What did the battery say to the corn chip?
  *"I'm Eveready. Are you Frito-Lay?"*

- What has eighteen legs and four tits?
  *The Supreme Court.*

- Why doesn't Santa Claus have any children?
  *Because he only comes once a year—and it's down a chimney.*

- Why did Lois Lane divorce Superman?
  *After he showed her his big red S, she found out that he was faster than a speeding bullet in bed, too.*

- Why did God make semen white and urine yellow?
  *So men could know the difference between coming and going.*

- What do you call the useless piece of skin attached to a penis?
  *A man.*

- Why do men like women who wear gold diaphragms?
  *Because they love coming into money.*

- Why did Bach have so many children?
  *Because he couldn't find the stops on his organ.*

- What's the square root of sixty-nine?
  *Ate something.*

- What did the girl potato say to the boy potato?
  *"Hey, you big spud. Would you like to climb into the sack with me?"*

- Why did the mother forbid her child to read *Ivanhoe*?
  *She heard it was full of Saxon violence.*

- How is sex like a bank?
  *Maturity yields increased interest, and there are substantial penalties for early withdrawal.*

- What do you call a woman without an asshole?
  *Single.*

- What did the hurricane say to the coconut palm?
  *"Hold on to your nuts. This ain't gonna be any ordinary blow job!"*

- What's the German word for a brassiere?
  *Holdsenfromfloppen.*

- What do you call a bunch of flat-chested shoppers?
  *A set of boobless buyers.*

- What do you call a magazine that features pictures of orgasms?
  *Spurts Illustrated.*

- What's wrinkled and smells like Ginger?
  *Fred Astaire's face.*

- How can you tell the head nurse?
  *The one with the dirty knees.*

- What did Snow White sing as she thought about making love to her prince?
  *"Someday my prince will come."*

- How many Californians does it take to screw in a lightbulb?
  *Californians don't screw in lightbulbs. They screw in hot tubs.*

- Why is the ERA an impossible dream?
  *Because there will always be a vas deferens between men and women.*

- Why is a Tampax like the starship *Enterprise*?
  *Because they both circle Uranus for Klingons.*

- Why did the dimwit staple his balls together?
  *He figured that if you can't lick 'em, you might as well join 'em.*

- What did Quakers used to say to each other when they got angry?
  *"Fuck thee!"*

- What did the leper say to the prostitute?
  *"You can keep the tip."*

- What do you get when you cross a virgin with a computer?
  *A system that won't go down.*

- What do you call a woman who performs marathon oral sex?
  *An all-day sucker.*

- What does LSMFT stand for?
  *"Let's stop. My finger's tired."*

- What do BS, MS, and PhD stand for?
  *"Bullshit," "More Shit," and "Piled Higher and Deeper."*

- What does ICBM stand for?
  *If it's a man, "Incredible Cock and Ball Machine"; if a woman, "Incredible Cunt and Boobs Machine."*

- What does OSIM stand for?
  *"Oh shit, it's Monday."*

- How do you remove semen from a condom?
  *Shake the fuck out of it.*

- What did the televangelist learn from the sex scandal that plunged him into disgrace?
  *Thou shalt not put thy rod into thy staff.*

- How is a paycheck like an erection in a woman's hand?
  *The more you work, the less you have to hold on to.*

- Why do women like Pac Man?
  *Where else can you get eaten three times for a quarter?*

- Why do big people make little people but big trains don't make little trains?
  *Because big trains always pull out on time.*

- What do you call a chain of hotel rooms where midgets can stay for nothing?
  *Stay-Free Mini Pads.*

- What makes a cannon roar?
  *You'd roar too if you had your balls shot off.*

What makes a cannon roar?

- How are women like pianos?
  *When they're not upright, they're grand.*

- What movie star has the dirtiest name?
  *Peter O'Toole.*

- What author has the dirtiest name?
  *John Fowles.*

- What football player has the dirtiest name?
  *Dick Butkus.*

- What planet has the dirtiest name?
  *Uranus.*

- What famous artist fingered his own bottom?
  *Pick-asso.*

- What do you call male prostitutes?
  *Peter Sellers.*

- What do you call money for the pay toilet?
  *Johnny Cash.*

- How did the American poet's lover introduce her to others?
  *"This is Edna St. Vincent, Millay."*

- What are the dirtiest words ever spoken on television?
  *"Ward, weren't you a little hard on the Beaver last night?"*

- What do you get when you goose a ghost?
  *A handful of sheet.*

- Which of the following doesn't belong?—eggs, rugs, meat, and a blow job?
  *A blow job. You can beat eggs and rugs, and you can beat your meat, but you can't beat a blow job.*

- How is life like a shit sandwich?
  *The more bread you have, the less shit you have to eat.*

- Why do women have two sets of lips?
  *So they can bitch and moan at the same time.*

- If nuts on a wall are called walnuts and nuts on a chest are called chestnuts, what do you call nuts on a chin?
  *A blow job.*

- Why did the attractive widow wear black garters?
  *They were in remembrance of those who had passed beyond.*

- Why do corporals have sex without rubbers?
  *Because they've read that syphilis is a disease of the privates.*

- What are two things in the air that can make a woman pregnant?
  *Her legs.*

- Why do basketball players make lousy lovers?
  *Because they always dribble before they shoot.*

- What do you call it when a man says to a woman, "Fuck you," and she replies, "Fuck you"?
  *Oral sex.*

- What's the cause of the population explosion?
  *Too many fucking people.*

- What do you call the children of prostitutes?
  *Brothel sprouts.*

- Why did the U.S. government use PMS women in the Persian Gulf in place of regular soldiers?
  *They're more vicious and they retain fluid.*

- Why do yuppie women postpone having children?
  *Because yuppie women never go into labor. They go directly into management.*

- What do you do in case of fallout?
  *Put it back in and take shorter strokes.*

- What's 6.9?
  *A delightful activity interrupted by a period.*

- What's 69 + 69?
  *Dinner for four.*

- What do you give to a man who has everything?
  *Penicillin.*

- Stop & Shop and A & P have decided to merge. What are they going to call the new conglomerate?
  *Stop & P.*

- How do you make vichyssoise?
  *First you take a leek . . .*

- Why did Josephine marry Napoleon?
  *She loved his bony part.*

- How is an ashtray like a toilet?
  *They're both places to put your butt in.*

- What do hard-of-hearing couples say to each other during intimate lovemaking?
  *"Come again?"*

- What did one shepherd say to the other shepherd?
  *"Lets get the flock out of here."*

- Why hasn't Barbie ever been pregnant?
  *Because Ken comes in a different box.*

- Why does the ocean roar?
  *You'd roar, too, if you had crabs on your bottom.*

- Why is a pool table green?
  *You'd be green too if someone was always racking your balls.*

- Why are schoolhouses red?
  *You'd be red too if you had six periods a day.*

- What did the woman say to her man when he sneezed as he penetrated her?
  *"Goes in tight!"*

- What did the Leaning Tower of Pisa say to Big Ben?
  *"If you've got the time, I've got the inclination."*

- What do you call an Eskimo who's a Peeping Tom?
  *An optical Aleutian.*

- Why is a high-priced call girl like a defense contractor?
  *They both charge $1,000 for a screw.*

- If an apple tree produces apples and a pear tree produces pears, what does a country produce?
  *Pussy willow.*

- How does a gynecologist greet a new acquaintance?
  *"Dilated to meet you. I've had a hard day at the orifice."*

- What do a lawyer and a sperm have in common?
  *They both have about a million-to-one chance of becoming a human being.*

- Why is a joke like a piece of ass?
  *Neither is any good if you don't get it.*

- Why is a joke like pussy?
  *Neither is any good if you don't get it.*

- What is every Amish woman's private fantasy?
  *Two Mennonites.*

- If Eve wore a fig leaf, what did Adam wear?
  *A hole in it.*

- Why are men like public toilets?
  *The good ones are taken, the rest are full of crap.*

- How did the Energizer Bunny die?
  *Somebody put his batteries in backward, and he kept coming, and coming, and coming.*

- What do you call an eighty-year-old impotent sailor?
  *A salt with a dead weapon.*

- What do you get when you cross an elephant with a prostitute?
  *A two-ton pickup.*

- What happened to the pope when he went to Mount Olive?
  *Popeye almost killed him.*

- What did Mr. Spock find in the restroom on the *Enterprise*?
  *The captain's log.*

- Why is 77 better then 69?
  *Because you get eight more.*

- Why does a one-story brothel make more money than a two-story brothel?
  *Because there's no fucking overhead.*

- What do bungee jumping and hookers have in common?
  *They both cost a hundred bucks, and if the rubber breaks, you're screwed.*

- Why don't rodeo cowboys make good lovers?
  *Because they think a good ride is eight seconds.*

- What has a whole bunch of little balls and screws old ladies?
  *A bingo machine.*

- What is safer, doing 69 or driving through fog?
  *Doing 69, that way you at least get to see the asshole in front of you.*

- What do you see when the Pillsbury Dough Boy bends over?
  *Donuts.*

- Why is it a mistake to date a necrophiliac?
  *He just wants you for your body.*

- What does an eighty-year-old woman taste like?
  *Depends.*

- What did Cinderella do when she got to the ball?
  *Gagged.*

- What do a tomcat on the prowl and a desperate poker player have in common?
  *They both put everything they have into the kitty.*

- What do a cheap hotel and tight jeans have in common?
  *No ballroom.*

- What's the first thing a sorority girl does in the morning?
  *Walks home.*

- Did you hear about the new blonde paint?
  *It's not real bright, but it's cheap, and spreads easy.*

- What's a blonde's favorite nursery rhyme?
  *Humpme Dumpme.*

- Lovers celebrate Valentine's Day. What do masturbators celebrate?
  *Palm Sunday.*

- What's it called when a woman is paralyzed from the waist down?
  *Marriage.*

# Risqué Business

A lawyer marries a woman who has previously divorced ten husbands.

On their wedding night she tells her new husband, "Please be gentle. I'm still a virgin."

"What?" asks the puzzled groom. "How can that be if you've been married ten times?"

"Well," she replies, "Husband number 1 was a sales representative. He kept telling me how great it was going to be.

"Husband number 2 was in software services. He was never really sure how it was supposed to function, but he said he'd look into it and get back to me.

"Husband number 3 was from field services. He said everything checked out diagnostically, but he just couldn't get the system up.

"Husband number 4 was in telemarketing. Even though he knew he had the order, he didn't know when he would be able to deliver.

"Husband number 5 was an engineer. He understood the basic process, but wanted three years to research, implement, and design a new state-of-the-art method.

"Husband number 6 was from finance and administration. He thought he knew how, but he wasn't sure whether it was his job or not.

"Husband number 7 was in marketing. Although he had a nice product, he was never sure how to position it.

"Husband number 8 was a psychiatrist. All he ever did was talk about it.

"Husband number 9 was a gynecologist. All he did was look at it.

"Husband number 10 was a stamp collector. All he ever did was . . . oh God, how I miss him!

"But now that I've married you, I'm really excited!"

"Good," says the lawyer, "but why?"

She replies, "Well, you're a lawyer. Now that I've married you, I know I'm gonna get screwed!"

In 1925 Calvin Coolidge declared that "the chief business of the American people is business." Judging from the number of dirty jokes that involve jobs and professions, it seems that the business of off-color humor is often business.

## *Par for the Coarse*

An American flies to Japan on a business trip. He's heard that Japanese women are very special in bed, so his first night in Tokyo he goes to a geisha house and hires out one of the girls. The whole time he's putting it to her she's yelling, "Fujigawa! Fujigawa!"

"Aha!" says the American. "I've just learned my first Japanese word. *Fujigawa* must mean 'great, wonderful, terrific.' I'll be sure to use it the first opportunity I get."

Turns out that the next morning he's out on a golf course playing a round with a Tokyo business contact. At the fourth tee the Japanese hits an incredible drive. The ball arcs beautifully, lands on the green, and rolls right into the cup for a hole-in-one. Seizing the opportunity, the American applauds and exclaims, "Fujigawa! Fujigawa!"

The Japanese turns to him and asks, "What you mean, 'wrong hole'?"

## The Facts About Safe Fax

Q. Do I have to be married to have safe fax?

A. Although married people fax quite often, there are many single people who fax complete strangers every day.

Q. My parents say they never had fax when they were young and were only allowed to write memos to each other until they were twenty-one. How old do you think someone should be before they can fax?

A. Faxing can be performed at any age, once you learn the correct technique.

Q. Can older people fax?

A. Despite myth, older people can fax as long as they can operate the equipment.

Q. If I fax to myself, will I go blind?

A. Certainly not, but, when you are older, you may have to wear glasses.

Q. There is a building on our street where you can go and pay to fax. Is this legal?

A. Yes, many people have no other outlet for their fax drives and must pay a professional when their need to fax becomes too great.

Q. Should a cover always be used for faxing?

A. Unless you are really sure of the one you are faxing, a cover should be used to ensure safe fax.

Q. What happens when my transmission is faulty and I fax prematurely?

A. Don't panic. Many people prematurely fax when they haven't faxed in a long time. Just start over—most people won't mind if you try again.

Q. I have a personal and a business fax. Can transmissions become mixed up?

A. Being bi-faxual can be confusing, but as long as you use a cover with each one, you won't transmit or receive anything you're not supposed to.

## In a Pickle

A man who works in a pickle factory develops an over-powering obsession to stick his penis in the pickle slicer. The obsession grows and grows and finally becomes a compulsion.

Finally, one day, right on the spot and in front of his fellow workers, he drops his pants and jams his penis right into the pickle slicer.

They fired him, of course—and they also fired the pickle slicer.

## Personnel Questions

A woman is being interviewed for a bank job by a personnel officer. He asks her a number of questions about her history and her qualifications, all the time filling in the blanks of the employment questionnaire:

"Name?"

"Jane Johnson."

"Age?"

"27."

"Sex?"

"Infrequently."

"Is that one word or two?"

## The Boss's Dilemma

The head of a small company has a problem. Business is bad, and it becomes absolutely necessary to reduce the staff by one employee. Jack Smith and Mary Jones are the two junior employees, and both are excellent workers. How, in all fairness, can the boss decide which one to fire?

Finally he hits upon the idea of letting luck decide. The next morning he keeps a close eye on the water cooler. Whichever of the two visit the cooler first will be the one to be let go.

Within an hour, Mary goes to the cooler for some water. The boss calls her into his office and explains, "Mary, I've got a terrible problem. I've either got to lay you or Jack off."

"Boss, I've got a pounding headache, so you'd better jack off."

## Plane Talk

A German-born rocket scientist, formerly an officer in the Luftwaffe, is the featured speaker at a NASA banquet. He reminisces about his wartime experiences as a pilot: "I was coming in on the Russians at twelve o'clock, high-strafing the bastards and dropping bombs at the same time. Well, two fuckers were supposed to be covering me at my right, when suddenly, I see this other fucker—"

The program chairman, an American general, interrupts smoothly, "Dr. Schiesskopf is referring of course to the old German fighter plane, the Fokker."

"No I'm not, General," returns the doctor. "That fucker was a Russian Mig!"

## Flight Instruction

As the airliner pushes back from the gate, the flight attendant gives the passengers the usual information regarding seat belts and safety, concluding with, "Please sit back and enjoy your trip while your captain, Martha Sperling, and crew take you safely to your destination."

Joe, sitting in the eighth row, thinks to himself, "Did I hear her right? Is the captain a woman? I think I better have a scotch and soda."

When the attendants come by with the drink cart, he asks, "Did I understand you right? Is the captain a woman?"

"Yes," replies the attendant. "In fact, this entire crew is female."

"My God," says Joe, "I'd better have two scotch and sodas. I don't know what to think of all those women up there in the cockpit."

"That's another thing," says the flight attendant. "We no longer call it the cockpit. It's now the box office."

## Short and Sweet

A newspaper editor is warned that he will be fired if he doesn't make his headlines more colorful and succinct. That night a sex maniac escapes from the local insane asylum and goes around having sex with laundry maids. For the news story that appears in the paper the next morning the editor writes this headline: NUT BOLTS, SCREW WASHERS.

## Sign Language

Two prostitutes are riding around town with a sign on top of their car that reads: TWO PROSTITUTES—$50.00.

A policeman stops them and tells them they have to remove the sign from their car. Just at that time, another car passes with a sign saying: JESUS SAVES.

One of the girls asks the cop, "How come you don't stop them?"

"Well, that's a little different," the cop smiles. "Their sign pertains to religion."

The following day finds the same cop in the area when he notices the two ladies of the evening driving around with a large sign on their car again. Figuring he has an easy arrest, he begins to catch up with them until he can read the new sign: TWO FALLEN ANGELS SEEKING PETER—$50.00.

## Giving Her the Business

A woman goes into a department store and tells the clerk that she wants to return a toaster for refund because it doesn't work.

The clerk tells her that he can't give her a refund because she bought it on special. All of a sudden the woman throws her arms up and yells, "Grab my breasts! Grab my breasts!"

The clerk doesn't know what to do so he calls the store manager, who asks her if he can help.

She explains that she wanted to return the nonworking toaster for a refund, and he tells her that he can't give her a refund because she bought the toaster on special.

Once again she yells, "Grab my breasts! Grab my breasts!"

The manager is taken aback and asks her why she was yelling that particular phrase. She replies, "Because I like my breasts grabbed when I'm getting screwed!"

## Playing It by Rear

Business is slow in the barroom when a bedraggled-looking fellow walks in and asks the bartender if he can play some songs on the piano. The bartender notices that the man's clothing is tattered to the point that his pants are ripped open and his balls are hanging out, but he still grants permission.

The man sits down and plays and sings with the talent of a seasoned entertainer. Soon a great crowd is attracted and business in the bar is booming.

In the middle of all this activity the bar's owner walks in and notices the man at the piano. "Hey, Joe," says the boss to the bartender, "that guy over there playing the piano is wearing clothes so torn that his balls are hanging out."

"I know," says Joe, "but I figured he was so good on the piano and was bringing in so many customers that I've let him stay."

"Well, maybe we can get him to change his clothes," says the owner and walks over to the piano player.

"Hey, mister, do you know your pants are ripped open and your balls are hanging out?"

"No, but if you hum it, I can play it."


## In a Wink

A fellow with long and varied experience with the ways of women goes into a whorehouse and asks the madam for a partner who can come up with something he's never tried before.

"That'll be Sadie on the fourth floor. If you're looking for something really new and different, try a wink job with her."

Not knowing what a wink job is, the man goes up to the fourth-floor room and meets Sadie. She's old, she's ugly, and, what's more, she's got a huge glass eye. Before the john can get out of the room, Sadie pulls out the eye and invites him to plant his love muscle in the concavity in her face. He does, she winks and winks away, and he experiences a thrill beyond any he's ever had before.

"That was incredible, Sadie," he thanks her. "I'll be back again for another one of those wink jobs."

"Any time, big boy," she says. "I'll be keeping an eye out for you."


## A Tacky Story

A man goes into a drugstore to buy a pack of condoms. When he pulls out his wallet to pay for his purchase, he notes that the bill is thirty-two cents higher than the price on the box. He asks why and is told that the extra money is for tax.

"Gee," he muses aloud. "I thought that you just rolled them on."

## See What I Mean?

Just as the smashing-looking woman emerges naked from the shower she hears a knock on her apartment door and a voice announce, "Blind man. I'm here to make a house call."

So instead of going back to the bathroom for her robe, she lets him in. On entering, the fellow can't stop staring at her striking and completely exposed figure.

"I thought you said you were the blind man!" she snaps.

"I am, and I'm here to fix your blinds."

## Happy Holiday

A Catholic chauffeur is talking with a friend about his Jewish employers. "Boy, do I have it made. They're really nice to me. They pay me well, and I get three weeks of vacation, in addition to all Jewish holidays like Rosh Hashanah."

"What's Rosh Hashanah?"

"That's the day they blow the shofar."

"Boy, you really do have it made!"

## The Great Dicktator

A man is dictating a telegram to his business partner by telephone: "Business is going very well. Stop. We need to order five thousand more widgets. Stop. Please send immediately. Stop."

"For God's sake, Charlie!" shouts the second man. "Will you please get your secretary to lay off you, and just dictate the order!"

## Door Prize

A woman goes to a hardware store and buys a hinge for a door.

"Wanna screw for it?" asks the salesman.

"No, but I'll blow you for a doorknob."

"I thought you said you were the blind man!"

## Superior Plans

The Mother Superior, as is her custom, interviews all of her young ladies about their plans for life after leaving the convent school. One announces that she hopes to become a nurse, another a teacher, and a third, hearing the call, has decided to stay on as a novice in the convent.

"And you?" asks the Mother Superior of the pretty girl who has remained silent.

"Oh, I want to become a prostitute, Mother Beatrice."

"What? You must be crazy! What did you say?"

"I said I want to be a prostitute."

"Oh, mother of Mary, thank the Lord, I thought you said you wanted to be a Protestant!"

## Three Cents' Worth

A customer in a restaurant leaves a measly three pennies as a tip. The waitress picks up the coins and says to the patron, "Using these three pennies, I can tell your fortune."

"OK, go ahead," he says.

She examines the first coin and says, "Well, this first penny tells me that you are a very frugal man."

"I sure am."

"The second penny tells me that you are single."

"Incredible! I am. How could you possibly know that?" the customer answers with some astonishment.

"And the third penny tells me that your father was also single."

## All Balled Up

Kramer receives an ad in the mail for a golf resort where everything costs one dollar. He jumps at the offer and heads off for a weekend of fun in the sun.

He arrives and plays a round of golf. It cost him a buck.

When he goes for dinner that evening, it costs him another buck.

His room is only a buck a day!

The day before he's to check out, he heads out to play a last round and stops by the pro shop and charges a sleeve of three balls to his room.

When he's checking out next morning, he looks at the bill and sees . . .

Golf: $1.00.

Dinner: $1.00.

Room: $1.00.

Sleeve of golf balls: $395.

He hits the ceiling!

Calling over to the manager, he asks, "What is this all about? Everything is supposed to cost one dollar, and you charged me $395 for three golf balls?"

"I'm sorry, sir," said the manager, "but you didn't read the fine print in our promotional brochure. That's what our golf balls cost."

"Well," said the man, "if I wanted to spend that kind of money, I could've gone to that luxury hotel across the street and paid them a $400 dollars a day for a room. At least I would've known what I was paying for!"

"That's right, sir, you could have," said the manager. "Over there they get you by the room. Over here we get you by the balls!"

## Sum Dum Fun

A Chinese couple who run a restaurant are asleep in bed. At three in the morning, the wife rolls over and whispers in her husband's ear, "I'd like some 69."

"Sorry, honey," he snorts. "We're out of egg foo yung."

As a public service, I offer their complete menu:

# Suc Mi Pagoda
### Cantonese Cuisine
6969 Fellatio Blvd. • Escondido, CA 12698
### 281-6969
*That's two ate one, sixty-nine, sixty-nine*

## A la Carte
### $2.69 each
1. Cum Drop Soup
   Fresh every 27 days
2. Pee Yu Platter
   Clothespins extra
3. Hoo Flung Dung
   Napkins and raincoats provided
4. Yung Poon Tang
   No take-out orders accepted
5. Chu Sum Twat
   Extra sauce provided

## Luncheon Specials
### $6.69 each
1. Sum Yung Chic
   Always freshly made
2. Won Hung Lo
   Chinese meatballs
3. Suc Sum Tit
   Boneless breast of chic
4. Wang Mi Butt
   A different approach
5. Suc Mi Pork
   Chef's special
6. Fuc Yu Mon
   Specialty of the house

## Dinner Combinations
### Includes smeg roll and fortune nookies

1. Goo In Hand ...............$9.69
   For those dining alone
2. Goo Wee Chic .............$6.69
   Sloppy seconds, no extra charge
3. Cum Tu Soon ...............$6.69
   Order early—these go fast
4. Suc Mi Dong ...............$6.69
   Traditional Chinese meatloaf
5. Sum Dum Fuc .............$2.69
   You get what you pay for
6. Fuc Yu Slo ...................$6.69
   Specialty of the house

7. Lik Mi Clit ..................$6.69
   A delicious, lip-smacking
   oriental delicacy
8. Cho Kon It .................$1.69
   Not for the lighthearted
9. Tung Sum Chic ..........$8.69
   A tastebud tingler
10. Wai Tu Yung ...............$4.69
    Not available on school nights
11. Fuc Sum Now ...........$7.69
    For those in a hurry
12. Sum Gulp Cum ..........$5.69
    Lo-cal special

### For Very Best Chow, You Cum Suc Mi Pagoda
Parking in Rear

## Quickies That Mean Business

- A man on a business trip went to a singles bar, approached two ladies, and offered either of them two hundred dollars to spend the night with him. One girl stormed out in a rage, but the other remained cool, calm, and collected.

- Motel 69: We leave the red light on for you.

- After auditioning for a part in a bikini commercial, the voluptuous blonde leaned over and told the producer, "If you're interested, you know where to get a hold of me."

# Have You Heard?

Have you heard about the virgin? She was impregnable, inconceivable, unbearable, unembeddable, impenetrable, insurmountable, impeccable, inscrutable—and ineffable.

Have you heard about the postman who was so popular with women? He was a first-class mail who made special deliveries with a lot of ZIP. He banged on the women's knockers and rang their bells. His leather sack was always bulging, and he slipped good things into their boxes. He always came twice a day, and he had the longest route in town.

Have you heard about the silly prostitute? She was always pulling boners. Have you heard about the bicentennial prostitute? She was an independent operator who charged 1776; it was a great deal, but she did it only with minutemen, and she yanked their doodles dandy. Have you heard about the blind prostitute? You really have to hand it to her. Have you heard about the broke prostitute? She said to her friend, "Can you lend me twenty bucks until I get back on my back again?"

Have you heard about the prostitute who decided to retire? She got tired of the hole business. Have you heard about the prostitute who got arrested? She wanted to be tried by the jury. Have you heard about the prostitute with a degree in psychology? She blows your mind. Have you heard about the prostitute who was into bondage? She was strapped for cash. Have you heard about the Apache prostitute? She did it for a hundred bucks. Have you heard about the prostitute who contracted appendicitis and they sewed up the wrong hole? Now she's making money on the side.

We live in a world of infinite variety, a planet populated by intriguing people and animals. Here are a number that you may not have heard about:

- Have you heard about the call girl who accidentally made two appointments at the same time?
  *She managed to squeeze them both in.*

- Have you heard about the sultan who had ten wives?
  *Nine of them had it pretty soft.*

- Have you heard about the Roman fighter with hair in his teeth?
  *He was gladiator.*

- Have you heard about the king who got shipwrecked on a desert island with no one but his court jester?
  *After a month the monarch was at his wit's end.*

- Have you heard about the exhibitionist who put off retirement?
  *He wanted to stick it out for another year.*

- Have you heard about the exhibitionist who went on trial?
  *He was taken into joint custody, but they couldn't make the evidence stand up in court. He was his own lawyer, and he got himself off.*

- Have you heard about the playboy meteorologist?
  *He could look at a woman and tell whether.*

- Have you heard about the nymphomaniacal dieter?
  *She was weighed in the balance and found wanton.*
- Have you heard about the liberated Irishwoman?
  *Her name was Erin Go Bra-less.*
- Have you heard about the horny Eskimo?
  *He was constantly cold-cocking his wife.*
- Have you heard about the woman who was half-Indian and half-Scottish?
  *She was a wonderful lay—both wild and tight.*
- Have you heard about the homeless snake?
  *He didn't have a pit to hiss in.*
- Have you heard about the uncircumcised troll?
  *His name was Rumpled Foreskin.*
- Have you heard about the masturbating Saxon?
  *His name was Onan the Barbarian.*
- Have you heard about the woman who bicycled over a long street of cobblestones?
  *She never came that way again.*
- Have you heard about the tone-deaf music critic?
  *He didn't know his brass from his oboe.*
- Have you heard about the successful burlesque queen?
  *She outstripped all her competitors.*
- Have you heard about the big-breasted woman?
  *Her men really had their hands full.*
- Have you heard about the astronaut who had sex with Venusians, Martians, and Jovians?
  *He was very good at spatial relations.*
- Have you heard about the wealthy robin?
  *It made a large deposit on a Rolls-Royce.*
- Have you heard about the firefly who backed into the candle?
  *He was de-lighted, no end.*

- Have you heard about the butcher who backed into the meat grinder?
  *He got a little behind in his work.*

- Have you heard about the woman who backed into the airplane propeller?
  *Disaster.*

- Have you heard about the cow who jumped over the barbed-wire fence?
  *Udder disaster.*

- Have you heard about the buxom soprano who fainted right in the middle of her aria?
  *It took four men to carry her from the stage—two abreast.*

- Have you heard about the voluptuous American girl who went to Paris to study?
  *She ended up with sore buns.*

- Have you heard about the vain plastic surgeon?
  *He went to his office and hung himself.*

- Have you heard about the virtuous millipede?
  *She crossed her legs and said, "No, no, a thousand times no!"*

- Have you heard about the fat lady who was arrested for drug smuggling?
  *During the search they lifted up her dress and found ten pounds of crack.*

- Have you heard about the woman who fell down on water skis?
  *She won the 100-yard douche.*

- Have you heard about the virginal man with thinning hair?
  *He hadn't gotten balled yet.*

- Have you heard about the moel who tried to circumcise himself?
  *He went off half-cocked.*

- Have you heard about the high-priced movie star?
  *He was always trying to make a little extra.*

- Have you heard about the girl named Virginia?
  *They called her Virgin for short—but not for long.*

- Have you heard about the fellow who sold padded bras door to door?
  *He was known as the Fuller Bust Man.*

- Have you heard about the female football player who became a prostitute?
  *She started as a tight end and finished as a split end and wide receiver. And her customers loved her because she never choked on the big ones.*

- Have you heard about the fly?
  *It was walking on a wall when it noticed that its man was open.*

- Have you heard about the narcoleptic playboy?
  *He always slept in snatches.*

- Have you heard about the deaf gynecologist?
  *He had to learn to read lips.*

- Have you heard about the prisoner who tried to get a female guard to help him escape?
  *He attempted to use a proposition to end a sentence with.*

- Have you heard about the fellow who went to Europe to have a sex change?
  *He got tired of the old joint.*

- Have you heard about the man with five penises?
  *His underwear fit him like a glove.*

- Have you heard about the new radio station—WPMS?
  *Each month it plays twenty days of easy listening, followed by five days of acid rock, followed by five days of ragtime.*

- Have you heard about the panty raid on the coven?
  *It was an embarrassment of witches.*

*The Fuller Bust Man*
Have you heard about the fellow
who sold padded bras door to door?

- Have you heard about the explosion in the fertilizer factory?
  *It created an offal smell.*

- Have you heard about the masseur who was fired from his job?
  *He kept rubbing his clients the wrong way.*

- Have you heard about the male and female ventriloquist's dummies?
  *They screwed their heads off.*

- Have you heard about the secretary who was making it with her boss when his wife walked in?
  *She had to change her position.*

- Have you heard about the fellow who wanted to get something for his wife?
  *He couldn't find anybody to make him an offer.*

- Have you heard about the woman who bought herself a slinky nightgown?
  *Her boyfriend tried to talk her out of it.*

- Have you heard about the woman who was fired from working at the sperm bank?
  *They caught her drinking on the job.*

- Have you heard about the cross-eyed seamstress?
  *She couldn't mend straight.*

- Have you heard about the three sailors who were walking along the beach?
  *A big WAVE came along and sucked them under the boardwalk.*

- Have you heard about the twenty-five-year-old woman who married an octogenarian?
  *Very soon she felt old age creeping up on her.*

- Have you heard about the movie star who lost popularity with his fans when he appeared in a blue movie?
  *They were disappointed with his small part.*

Have you heard about
the male and female ventriloquist's dummies?
They screwed their heads off.

- Have you heard about the two nudists who split up?
  *They were seeing too much of each other.*

- Have you heard about the man who lost the light of his life?
  *He found a new match.*

- Have you heard about the woman who made love with a ghost?
  *She didn't know she had it in her.*

- Have you heard about the couple who had a platonic relationship?
  *For him it was play; for her it was tonic.*

- Have you heard about the lisping shoe salesman?
  *He was always trying to look up a woman's thize.*

- Have you heard about the woman who married a fellow named William so that she would have a Will of her own?
  *Then she married a guy named Richard.*

- Have you heard about the all-female hockey team?
  *They're called the Motherpuckers, and they change their puds after every period.*

- Have you heard about the nymphomaniacal bank robber?
  *She blew the safe and then went down on the elevator.*

- Have you heard about the one-legged virgin?
  *Her name was Hopalong Chastity.*

- Have you heard about the fellow who was delivering an outhouse?
  *He had a good head on his shoulders.*

- Have you heard about the king of Sodom and Gomorrah?
  *Herpes II.*

- Have you heard about the new universities that have been built in Egypt, Iran, and Utah?
  *Farouk U, Ayatollah U, and Friggem Young.*

- Have you heard about the promiscuous coed?
  *While others were dissecting frogs, she was opening flies.*

- Have you heard about the randy priest?
  *He was a sinner qua nun. In the monastery he was constantly trying to get into the habit. When he did, he always waited for the second coming.*

- Have you heard about the nymphomaniac who died during an ocean crossing?
  *She tried to go down on the* Titanic.

- Have you heard about the sentimental moel?
  *He was a skinflint who saved all his clippings.*

- Have you heard about the contortionist who became a hermit?
  *He learned to live alone and lick it.*

- Have you heard about the illegitimate Rice Krispie?
  *It had snap, it had krackle, but no pop.*

- Have you heard about the woman who married a fighter pilot?
  *She wanted to have an ace in the hole.*

- Have you heard about the nymphomaniacal Mensan?
  *She's a fucking know-it-all.*

- Have you heard about the gigolo in the leper colony?
  *Everything was fine until his business started falling off.*

- Have you heard about the woman who came over to look at her boyfriend's unfurnished apartment?
  *She was floored.*

- Have you heard about the woman who had intercourse only with oversexed men?
  *She didn't have a lazy bone in her body.*

- Have you heard about the woman who had sex with a racehorse?
  *She's now in a stable condition.*

- Have you heard about the woman who gave her first blow job?
  *It had never entered her head before.*

- Have you heard about the farmer who couldn't keep his hands off his wife?
  *He had to fire them all.*

- Have you heard about the home-loving girl?
  *She did some loving in the car, too.*

- Have you heard about the musical ensemble that performed sex on stage?
  *It's called the Coitus String Quartet.*

- Have you heard about the amorous dove?
  *She often got pigeonholed.*

- Have you heard about the pregnant unwed mother?
  *Nobody could figure out what had gotten into her.*

- Have you heard about the fellow who had sex almost every day?
  *He almost had it on Monday, almost had it on Tuesday . . .*

- Have you heard about the all-female professional wrestling circuit?
  *It's motto was "No holes barred."*

- Have you heard about the man who had a model penis?
  *The dictionary defines "model" as "a small imitation of the real thing."*

- Have you heard about the fellow who had syphilis, gonorrhea, and herpes?
  *He was an incurable romantic.*

- Have you heard about the oversexed woman who would take her vibrator into the tanning booth?
  *She loved to shake and bake.*

Have you heard about the farmer who couldn't keep his hands off his wife?

- Have you heard about the man who liked bathing beauties?
  *He bathed at least one a week.*

- Have you heard about the new feminine hygiene deodorant named SSY?
  *It takes the PU out of PUSSY.*

- Have you heard about the eighty-year-old man who woke up one morning feeling like an eighteen-year-old?
  *Unfortunately, he couldn't find one that early.*

- Have you heard about the couple who always showered before having intercourse?
  *They wanted to come clean.*

- Have you heard about the fat whore who retired?
  *Her departure left a big hole to fill.*

- Have you heard about the cannibal who always ate everything that was placed on his plate?
  *He had a ball.*

- Have you heard about the woman who wore atomic dresses?
  *They were mostly fallout.*

- Have you heard about the kept woman?
  *She wears mink all day and fox all night.*

- Have you heard about the nymphomaniac who became a trainer for a professional football team?
  *She kept pulling the players' muscles.*

- Have you heard about the fellow who couldn't distinguish between a Muslim and shoe polish?
  *He didn't know Shiite from Shinola.*

- Have you heard about the miserly customer at the whorehouse?
  *He'd always dicker before he'd dick her.*

- Have you heard about the rancher who let his cows roam anywhere they wished?
  *He let the chips fall where they may.*

- Have you heard about the nymphomaniacal philosopher?
  *Her name was Simone de Boudoir.*

- Have you heard about the two writers who collaborated on a book about sanitary napkins?
  *They were coauthors of a cotext.*

- Have you heard about the woman whose boyfriend asked her if they could move from having a PG to an R relationship?
  *She shot him.*

- Have you heard about the cockney prostitute?
  *She was known as the London derriere.*

- Have you heard about the constipated mathematician?
  *He worked it out with a slide rule.*

- Have you heard about the ass-licking comedian?
  *His humor was tongue-in-cheek.*

- Have you heard about the urologist who was sued for malpractice?
  *He was tried before a jury of his pee'ers.*

- Have you heard about the nearsighted woman?
  *She couldn't tell her friends until they were right on top of her.*

- Have you heard about the nymphomaniacal Israelite?
  *She was always trying to make a prophet.*

- Have you heard about the fellow who had a relationship with an Eskimo woman?
  *All went well, until she broke it off.*

- Have you heard about the downhill skier who was an exhibitionist?
  *They arrested him for in-descent exposure.*

- Have you heard about the new airline for old people?
  *It's called Incontinental.*

- Have you heard about the new blond paint?
  *It's not very bright, but it's cheap and spreads easily.*

- Have you heard about the new all-female delivery service?
  *It's called U.P.M.S. They will deliver your parcel when they are fucking ready.*

- Have you heard about the blonde who had two chances to get pregnant?
  *She blew it both times.*

- Have you heard about the lady who had a successful career as a dancer?
  *She didn't dance very well on her left leg and she didn't dance very well on her right leg, but between the two of them she made a very good living.*

- Have you heard about the constipated composer?
  *He couldn't finish the last movement.*

- Have you heard about the constipated accountant?
  *He couldn't budget.*

- Have you heard about the latest contraceptive for men?
  *It's called the contraceptive burr. He puts it in his shoe and it makes him limp.*

- Have you heard about the new douche they've made for women?
  *It's made of marijuana, Arrid, and Kentucky Fried Chicken. It leaves you high, dry, and fingerlicking good.*

# Graphic
# Humor

A metropolitan library commissions a famous modern artist to paint a mural depicting Custer's last stand. He sequesters himself for months working on the painting, and finally the day of the unveiling arrives. The distinguished guests and a bevy of reporters and photographers stand ready, and the cloth is drawn back from the mural.

A great gasp escapes from those assembled. Men cover their eyes, women faint, and a near riot ensues. In the middle of the mural is pictured a large cow with a halo floating above her head. On the ground around the bovine are piles of cowflop. Above each steaming mass is suspended a halo. And encircling the cow are couple after couple of copulating Indians.

After the initial shock has dissipated, the art critic for the *New York Times* clears his throat and summons up the courage to ask the artist, "Could you please tell us what you are trying to say with the imagery you have created in your painting?"

"Sure," replies the painter. "You see, I am trying to depict what words went through General Custer's head at the exact moment that he and his troops came over the hill at Little Big Horn."

"And what were those words?"

"Holy cow! Holy shit! Look at all those fucking Indians!"

The painter is thrown into jail for ten years. When he's released, a famous music conservatory in a faraway city, not having heard about the first scandal, asks him to produce a mural depicting his favorite piece of music.

Again the artist labors in seclusion for months. Again the big day arrives. Again the curtain is drawn back. Again there is deep shock, and again men cover their eyes and women faint.

This time the artist has painted seven naked and buxom women lined up in a row. The first, third, fifth, sixth, and seventh of the women are bending over and mooning the viewer, while the second and fourth are thrusting forward their generous tits.

After another near riot, the painter is again asked to explain his concept. "No problem," he expostulates. "What you see here is a graphic display of the *William Tell Overture.*"

*"For the benefit of those of us who are not conversant in artistic theory, could you please tell us how in the world these seven nudes can represent the William Tell Overture?"* asks one of the reporters.

"Rump, titty, rump, titty, rump, rump, rump."

For more picturesque humor, continue on through the rest of this chapter, where you will find a gallery of graphic depictions by my immensely talented and filthy-minded artist, Dave Morice:

An Ass

A Back Side

Balls

A Bang

A Beaver

A Bitch

A Blow Job

Boobs

A Box

Buns

A Butt

A Cat House

A Cherry

The Clap

A Cock

Craps

A Dick

An Erection

A Fly

A Good Lay

A Goose

A Honeypot

A Hooker

Horny

Hot to Trot

A Hump

Intercourse

A Joint

Jugs

Melons

Nuts

An Organ

**Passing Gas**

**A Pecker**

**A Period**

**A Piece of Tail**

A Prick

Privates

A Pussy

Road Apples

A Rod

A Roll in the Hay

Screwing

The Shaft

Sixty-Nine

A Snatch

A Tit

A Tool

A Trick

A Weenie

Well Hung

A Wet Spot

# Interlewd

### An Old Joke

An eighty-five-year-old man and an eighty-two-year-old woman become friends in a retirement home. After several months they agree to meet in her room to see if they, in their sere and yellow leaf of life, can still have sexual intercourse.

They both undress and the woman says to the man, "Before we start, I must warn you that I have acute angina."

"I do hope so," says the man. "Because your tits are sure ugly."

### A Moody Story

One Halloween a society hostess puts on a masquerade ball, and she asks all who attend to dress up as emotions. One man comes dressed all in green. "You are dressed to look like envy," everyone guesses correctly.

A woman arrives in an all-blue costume. "You're supposed to be sadness," the crowd surmises.

Late in the evening a man enters. He wears no costume; in

fact, he's stark naked, and his dick is immersed in a bowl of pudding. "What emotion could you possibly be?" wonder his friends.

"Anger. I'm fuckin' dis custard!"

## Fits to a T

A man on a plane finds himself sitting next to a strikingly beautiful and well-endowed young woman who is wearing a T-shirt with "NAN" emblazoned across the front.

To break the ice, he turns to her and asks, "Excuse me, is your name Nan?"

"Why, no," she answers. "Whatever made you think that my name is Nan?"

"Because of those letters on your shirt—NAN."

"Oh, now I see. But actually NAN stands for 'National Association of Nymphomaniacs.' I'm a member, and I'm just coming back from our annual conference."

"Wow!" exclaims the man, taken aback. "I didn't know that there was an organization for nymphomaniacs. Tell me, what do you do at your meetings?"

"We have some very interesting and intellectual discussions. The last seminar I attended we talked about the kinds of men that nymphomaniacs are attracted to."

"And what did you decide?" asks the man, leaning forward with increasing interest.

"We concluded that there are two kinds of men that are most attractive to nymphomaniacs—cowboys and Jewish men."

"That's fascinating. Please allow me to introduce myself. My name is Hopalong Goldberg."

## Fairy Tales Can Come True

Truth be told, Cinderella is the most promiscuous piece of fairy tail in the whole kingdom. She lets Jack be nimble and quick with her and Little Jack Horner stick his thumb into her plum.

One day Cindy's fairy godmother appears and screams, "Cinderella, if you don't stop screwing everyone in Fairyland, you'll never get to ball with the prince. To protect you, I'm going to turn your pussy into a pumpkin!" And, waving her magic wand—zap!—that's just what she does.

A month later, the godmother pays Cinderella another visit to see how her presumably celibate charge is doing. The old woman is surprised to see Cinderella smiling broadly and dancing about the house.

"What are you smiling about?" asks the godmother.

"I've met a wonderful new man. His name is Peter, Peter . . ."

## The Seduction

"Oh John, please don't park."

"Oh John, please don't."

"Oh John, please."

"Oh John."

"Oh."

## Low-Grade Humor

"Mommy, how old are you?" asks a ten-year-old boy.

"Now Willie, little boys don't ask their mothers their age."

"Mommy, how much do you weigh?"

"Willie, that's another question that little boys shouldn't be asking their mothers."

"Well, Mommy, why are you and Daddy thinking about getting a divorce?"

"Willie! That's definitely a question that little boys should never ask their mothers!" And she throws him out of the room.

A week later little Willie finds his mother's driver's license lying on her bureau. He sits down and reads it, and the next time Willie and his mother are together alone, he says, "Mommy, I know how old you are. You're forty-two."

"Well, yes, Willie, that's what I am."

"Mommy, I know that you weigh 136 pounds."

"Incredible! That is what I weigh!"

"And Mommy, I know why Daddy and you are thinking about getting a divorce."

"Huh? Why?" asks the astonished mother.

"Because you got an 'F' in 'Sex'!"

## I Love What You Do to Me

A woman spends an hour in the supermarket doing an enormous shopping. Shortly after she wheels her heavily laden shopping cart through the door and out onto the pavement, an attendant comes up and offers to take the cart to her car and to put the bags in the trunk.

This kid is a real hunk—6'2", well-muscled body, blue eyes, and blond hair, and the woman gets hot to trot and purrs to the boy, "Young man, I've got an itchy pussy."

"Sorry, lady," he says. "All those Japanese cars look the same to me. What color is yours?"

## I'll Drink to That

HILLBILLY BOY: "Maw! I've just picked up a case of VD!"

MAW: "Put it in the basement. Your paw'll drink anything!"

## Fuzz Buster

HIPPIE: "Say, honey, have you ever been picked up by the fuzz?"

HIPPETTE: "No, but I've been twirled by the tits."

## So What Else Is New?

HUSBAND TO WIFE: "How about a little action tonight, honey?"

WIFE: "Over my dead body!"

HUSBAND: "How else?"

"Maw! I've just picked up a case of VD!"

## Hard of Herring

A woman riding in a Boston taxi asks the driver where she can get scrod. "I didn't know that the verb had that past tense," mutters the cabbie.

## Woden You Know It?

Thor grows tired of drinking mead in the land of the Scandinavian gods, so he pays a visit to Earth. He soon meets a scullery maid and takes her to bed. After four hot and heavy days and nights, Thor decides to go back to Valhalla. But before departing, he wishes to explain to the girl how lucky she has been to have made love with a god. "I'm Thor," he informs her.

"You think *you're* thor. I'm tho thor I can't even pith."

## Petered Out

A virgin dies and goes to heaven, where she meets St. Peter. "You have led a good and virtuous life," says the Pearly Gate-keeper, "but before you can enter heaven, you must answer one question correctly."

"I'll try," says the virgin.

St. Peter asks, "What were Adam's first words to Eve?"

"Oh boy, that's a hard one."

"You're right! Now enter the gates of heaven!"

## Long Division

A middle-aged couple are discussing their plans for the future. "When I'm eighty," says the man to his wife, "I plan on finding myself a pretty twenty-year-old, and we'll live it up together." Only temporarily taken aback, the wife replies, "When I'm eighty, I plan on finding myself a handsome twenty-year-old. Twenty goes into eighty a lot easier than eighty goes into twenty."

## One for the Road

A woman comes into a restaurant and strikes up a conversation with a fellow at the bar. They hit it off fine, and he suggests that they continue the repartee with a drink at his place.

She accepts but warns him. "All right, but I must caution you that I'm on my menstrual cycle."

To which he replies, "No problem. I'll just follow you in my Honda."

## An Electrifying Tale

One night when his charge was exceptionally high, Micro Farad, a real-time operator and habitual multiuser, decided to seek out a cute little piece of liveware to help him discharge. He picked up Millie Amp and took her for a ride on his megacycle. They rode out to the beach to watch the magnetic waves.

"How are you, Honeywell?" Micro inquired.

"I'm kind of down because I've been dumped recently," replied Millie.

Attracted by Millie Amp's user-friendliness and characteristic curves, Micro was soon fully charged with attraction. Using his magnetic personality, he removed his shorts, laid her on the ground potential, lowered her resistance, and raised her frequency. Hoping to socket to her but not be charged with battery, he pulled out his high-voltage probe, connected them in parallel, entered his data in her software, and began short-circuiting her resistance shunt.

Growing tensor and tensor, he kept on plugging as the electrified Millie moaned, "Get BASIC with me! RAM me! OHM my! MHO, MHO, give me MHO!"

With his hardware and shielded tube operating at maximum peak and her wetware and field vibrating with his current flow, Millie Amp soon reached her saturation point, and Micro Farad rapidly discharged, draining every electron. All night they fluxed, trying various connections until his magnet had a soft core and lost all its field strength.

Afterwards, Millie Amp tried self-induction and damaged her solenoid. With his battery fully discharged, Micro Farad was unable to excite his generator. So they spent the rest of the night reversing polarity and blowing each other's fuses.

### Sibling Bribery

The little brother rebuffs all offers of money to leave the parlor so that his sister and her boyfriend can pet. "What do you want?" the exasperated sister finally asks.

"I wanna watch."

So they let him.

### Wishful Thinking

A pair of stage-door Johnnies are ogling the cuties who are leaving the dressing rooms.

"Do you see that redhead over there? I feel like screwing her again."

"Wow! You mean to tell me that you've been doing it with that great-looking piece of ass?"

"No, I felt like it before, and I feel like it now."

### Getting to the Bottom of the Problem

The couple is out having a sumptuous dinner when she starts choking on a piece of food. He immediately tears off her dress and runs his tongue vigorously along her bottom.

Despite his weird behavior, she recovers quickly and berates him for his obscene actions. "But I was just administering the Heine Lick Maneuver," he explains.

### A Weighty Matter

The male bodybuilder eyed a gorgeous female lifting weights in the gym. He ambled over and said, "Hey, babe. What do you say to a little private training session?"

She replied, "What do you have in mind?"

He stared at her crotch and leered, "I feel like working on the snatch."

She retorted, "I think you should head for the showers."

"Why?"

She pointed at his crotch and said, "You'll have to settle for the clean and jerk."

## The Cover-up

"But my elderly aunt was considered a highly respectable spinster!" the society matron protested. "Can't you find some way to cover up the shocking fact that she died in bed while being simultaneously serviced by two paid studs?"

"You just leave it to me, Mrs. Van Horn," soothed the police officer. "I'll just put it in my report that she died at the stroke of two."

## Titillating Labeling

The success of the Wonder Bra for underendowed women has encouraged the designers to come out with a bra for over-endowed women. It's called the Sheep Dog Bra. It rounds them up and points them in the right direction.

• Ever wonder why ABCDEF are used to define bra sizes?

    A = Almost
    B = Better
    C = Cute
    D = Damn good
    E = Enormous
    F = Fake

And for the fifty-and-over group:

    G = Gone south

## A Hairy Encounter

One evening the Wolfman comes home from a long day at the office.

"How was work, dear?" his wife asks.

"Listen! I don't want to talk about work!" he shouts.

"Okay. Would you like to sit down and eat a nice home-cooked meal?" she asks nicely.

"I'm not hungry!" he snarls. "I don't wanna eat! Is that all right with you? Can I come home from work and just do my own thing without you forcing food down my throat? Huh!"

Then Wolfman starts growling and throwing things around the apartment in a titanic rage.

Looking out the window, his wife sees a full moon and says to herself, "Well, I guess it must be that time of the month."

## Not in the Swim

Greta enters an important breaststroke competition. The starting gun goes off, and, while all the other contestants plunge into the pool and flail through the water, Greta simply floats face-down on the surface.

Of course Greta finishes two hours behind all the other swimmers, and one conscientious reporter has waited to interview her. "Greta, why did you simply float while all the others swam the breaststroke?"

"Those women cheated! Nobody told me you could use your arms!"

## Tea for Two

On an airplane an Englishman and a Texan get into a conversation about tea.

"In England, we have many kinds of tea," boasts the English fellow. "We have herbal tea, which is 80 percent aroma and 20 percent substance, and robust tea, which is 20 percent aroma and 80 percent substance. But the best tea is the queen's tea, which is what I drink."

"Well," drawls the Texan, "we've got all kinds of tea in Texas, too. There's f-a-r-tea, which is 80 percent aroma and 20 percent substance, and s-h-i-tea, which is 20 percent aroma and 80 percent substance. But the best tea is c-u-n-tea, which is what I drink."

## Dream On

HE: "I had a dream about you last night."
SHE: "Did you?"
HE: "No, you wouldn't let me."

## Triple Play

The new mother of triplets gushes proudly, "And just think, it happens only once in every 185,875 times!"

"That's wonderful," agrees her friend. "But I don't see how you find time for housework."

## In the Line of Duty

A soldier, commended for extreme bravery on the front, is coming home to his family. His little son looks out the window and sees his father walking up the path to the front door. "Look, Mommy," the boy exclaims, "Daddy's got a Purple Heart on!" "I've been waiting so long to see him," the mother smiles, "I don't care what color it is."

## Weather or Not

"How the hell should I know!" shrieks the husband into the phone. "Why don't you call the Weather Bureau?"

"Who's that on the phone?" asks his wife.

"I don't know. Just some damn fool wanting to know if the coast is clear."

## Problems, Problems

A problem recently developed at a coeducational college. Forty of the female students exhibited the effects of severe lack of sleep.

The school's physicians, psychiatrists, and psychologists were asked to try to solve the problem, but they were stumped. Finally the head of the math department stepped forward and proclaimed, "Anything can be resolved with mathematics." Then he proceeded to write this formula:

S L E E P + N I G H T = 40 women
0 1 2 3 4   5 6 7 8 9

"Now," he continued, "select any three digits as they appear in order, such as 123 or 678. Let's take 567. Reverse the sequence and subtract the smaller from the larger:

$$\begin{array}{r} 765 \\ -567 \\ \hline 198 \end{array}$$

"Reverse that number and this time add the two:

$$\begin{array}{r} 198 \\ +891 \\ \hline 1{,}089 \end{array}$$

"Now multiply this figure by forty women, then substitute the letter appearing above each number in the formula. The result will tell you what is keeping the women awake."

# What Do You Call a Sex Pack?

Five Oxford University dons are strolling the Oxford streets one evening and heatedly discussing some arcane aspect of group nouns, such as a *gaggle of geese, a covey of quail,* and a *pride of lions.* As they expostulate, they spy, coming at them, a small but conspicuous group of prostitutes.

One of the dons turns to the others and asks, "What would you call *them?*"

The first, a master of culinary arts, offers "a jam of tarts."

The second, a fellow in music, rejoins "a flourish of strumpets."

From the third, an expert in nineteenth-century literature, comes "an essay of Trollope's."

The fourth—twentieth-century literature—ripostes "an anthology of pros."

The fifth, the dean of the dons and senior master in zoology, closes the game with "a pride of loins."

But not closed—no. For the five pedagogues have only begun to tap this rich vein of bawdy gold.

Read on.

a column of figures

a pot of flesh

a school of scandals

a chamber of whores

a turning of screws

a rumble of seat

a farm of fannies

a pyre of vamps

a bowl of cherries

a steamer of tramps

a can of manhandlers

a set of wenches

a soup of wantons

a stack of dishes

a comb of honeys

a plague of low cuts

a bench of solicitors

an expanse of broads

an attack of vaginas

a peal of Jezebels

a handful of claps

a flock of swallows

a staff of infection

a frosting of hoars

a service of prosses

a heaving of thighs

a demonstration of piece

a vile of crack

a covey of tail

a casting of hookers

a shot of courtesans

an explosion of bangs

a bag of tricks

a swarm of B's

a suckling of pigs

a giggle of goose

a gift of grab

a melody of snatch

a range of mounts

a flotilla of carriers

a troop of pickups

a cantata of box

a garland of lays

a popping of turnovers

a contract of breaches

an infinitive of splits

a crook of buy hookers

a tour of pro-ballers

A set of wenches

a trap of boobies

a suite of orifices

a bramble of bush

a clutch of beavers

a prickle of concubines

a litter of pussy

a caravan of asses

a catch of clams

a pinch of crabs

a twitter of tits

a dawning of cracks

a parade of beefeaters

a side of rump

an asstray of butts

a standing of ovulation

a twattle of busy bodies

Still not closed, for men, too, are fit subjects for the same kind of verbal virtuosity. You see, all along, while the Oxford scholars were bantering about their group nouns, the ladies of the evening were inventing their own linguistic labels for the race of grand pricks coming *their* way:

a kit of tools

a coil of hoses

a totem of poles

a flush of johns

a drive of screwers

a round of set-ups

a ram of rods

a rod of rams

a battery of testes

a modem of wangs

a smoking of joints

a stand of timber

a dangling of participles

a turning of cranks

an excitement of uprisings

a smorgasbord of meats

a barrel of pork

an elevation of shafts

a rooting of hogs

a posting of male

an exhibit of bones

a bouquet of orchids

a phalanx of pikes

a bluff of poker

a deck of cads

a belt of studs

a tinkling of jewels

a plot of thickening

a symphony of organs

a bunch of miss-fits

a mass of cunt-fusion

a flurry of blows

a case of lickers

a cirrhosis of lovers

a statue of libertines

a procession of penetrants

a party of congressmen

a heartbreak of satyriasis

a withering of heights

a battalion of privates

a bob of comings

an affirmation of oui-ouis

a ring of ding-dongs

a fort of dicks

an assortment of nuts

a hollow of weenies

a doodling of cocks

a firm of members

a set of erections

a protrusion of high-rises

an erection of condominiums

an outpost of syphilisation

a peck of peters

a peter of peckers

a circle of jerks

a fold of foreskins

a play of glandstands

a drop of whorehounds

a volley of balls

an exclamation of points

a dinghy of semen

a whale of sperm

a sinking of putz

a wonderland of phalluses

# Delectable Daughters

In *Word Play,* Peter Farb explains that "the majority of American children are strikingly punctual in acquiring a repertoire of riddles at about age six or seven." What Farb doesn't say is that children are also strikingly punctual about acquiring a repertoire of off-color jokes, and many of these are built on certain popular formulas.

My own youthful collection included a library shelf of book-and-author jokes, among them:

*The Tiger's Revenge,* by Claude Balls

*The Man with No Pecker,* by I. Kutchacockoff

*The Yellow Stream,* by I. P. Daily

*I Love Virgins,* by Buster Highman

*The Breast,* by I. Suckatitski

*The Strange Scrotum,* by Won Hung Lo

*The Brown Apartment,* by Hu Flung Dung

Then there was the "Confucius-say" series:

- Man who make love with woman on top is always fucking up.
- Woman who stand behind male quartet, she behind eight ball.
- Man who kisses ass is bound to get shitfaced.
- Woman who wear glass diaphragm, she have womb with a view.
- Man who read women like books enjoy the climax best.
- Woman perched on sex fiend is sitting in the lap of lechery.
- Man who farts in church sits in his own pew.
- Woman who boils cabbage and peas in same pot is unsanitary.
- Man who screws girlfriend in country has found piece on earth.
- Man with athletic finger often make broad jump.
- Woman who use Crisco get fat in can.
- Man who goes to sleep with sex problem often wake up with solution in hand.
- Abstinence makes the tart go yonder.
- Kiss that speaks volumes is seldom first edition.
- Secretary not permanent unless screwed on desk.
- Man who loses key to girlfriend's apartment will not get any new key for awhile.
- Seven-day honeymoon make one hole weak.

"Never say die" jokes seem never to say die. When General Douglas MacArthur retired from military life in 1951, he declaimed the famous line, "Old soldiers never die—they just fade away." But five-star army generals aren't the only ones who never say die. Little did MacArthur know that he had started a new trend in suggestive humor:

- Old statisticians never die. They just get broken down by age, sex, and marital status.
- Old classicists never die. First they conjugate. Then they decline.
- Old rabbis never die. They just get gray around the temples and balled in the middle.
- Old truckers never die. They just get a new Peterbilt.

And, of course, childhood opened the door to a number of punographic knock-knock jokes:

> Knock, knock.
> Who's there? Marmalade.
> Marmalade who?
> Marmalade a baby.

> Knock, knock.
> Who's there?
> Fornication.
> Fornication who?
> Fornication like this I'll have to wear a tuxedo.

> Knock, knock.
> Who's there?
> Argo.
> Argo who?
> Argo fuck yourself!

> Knock knock.
> Who's there?
> Dictaphone.
> Dictaphone who?
> Dictaphone up your ass!

Perhaps the most fruitful of all foul formula jokes is the "She was only a _____'s daughter, and _____" routine:

- She was only an optician's daughter, and she certainly could make a spectacle of herself.

- She was only a circus clown's daughter, and her loving was sure in tents.

- She was only a taxidermist's daughter, and she often got stuffed and mounted.

- She was only a fisherman's daughter, and when she saw a man's rod, she reeled. And she loved a cockle mussel—just for the halibut.

- She was only a wallflower's daughter, and she was dandelion in bed.

- She was only a mason's daughter, and she got laid up and down the block.

- She was only a swimmer's daughter, and she knew every dive in town.

- She was only a farmer's daughter, and she was the best little hoer in the county.

- She was only a dentist's daughter, and everybody wanted to fill her cavity.

- She was only a rancher's daughter, and she couldn't keep her calves together.

- She was only a realtor's daughter, and she gave lots away.

- She was only a golf pro's daughter, and she showed the old duffers how to get out of the rough and sink their putts into the hole.

- She was only a stableman's daughter, and all the horsemen knew her.

- She was only a pianist's daughter, and when she wasn't up-right, she was grand.

- She was was only a poet's daughter, and she sure liked a Longfellow.

- She was only a jockey's daughter, and she often got bedridden bareback.

- She was only a coach's daughter, and she always made the team.

- She was only a cheerleader's daughter, and she sure made the boys' root harder.

- She was only a cyclist's daughter, and she peddled it all over town.

- She was only an ornithologist's daughter, and, with her parakeets, she loved to play with a cockatoo.

- She was only an archer's daughter, and her sheath made men quiver.

- She was only an apple-grower's daughter, and she couldn't wait to get it in cider.

- She was only a pirate's daughter, and she had a sunken chest.

- She was only a baker's daughter, and, with her buns, she sure made one hell of a turnover.

- She was only a janitor's daughter, and she was often swept off her feet.

- She was only a sailor's daughter, and she often put out to see.

- She was only a dollmaker's daughter, and she closed her eyes when you laid her down.

- She was only a mathematician's daughter, and she sure learned how to multiply using square roots.

- She was only a photographer's daughter, and she loved to develop things in a dark room.

- She was only a filmmaker's daughter, and she often ended up on the cutting-room floor.

- She was only a telephone operator's daughter, and she became a call girl who never gave a busy signal.

- She was only a grammarian's daughter, and she never declined and always conjugated. In fact, she was often caught with dangling participles.

- She was only a moonshiner's daughter, and the mountin' men loved her still.

- She was only a carillonneur's daughter, and she became the village belle with quite a clapper.

- She was only an Australian's daughter, and she often got explored Down Under.

- She was only a postman's daughter, and she got a lot of male in her box.

- She was only a tailor's daughter, and she sure could give tit for tat.

- She was only a clergyman's daughter, and she always did it religiously—on her knees.

- She was only a church musician's daughter, and she loved to catch hims by the organ.

- She was only a mechanic's daughter, and she was awfully auto-erotic.

- She was only an electrician's daughter, and she made house calls to remove her customers' shorts.

- She was only a hardware store owner's daughter, and she worked with nuts and screws.

- She was only a florist's daughter, and whenever she was potted she got deflowered.

- She was only a boxer's daughter, and boy could she Everlast.

She was only a florist's daughter, and whenever she was
potted she got deflowered.

- She was only a hunter's daughter, and she sure was fair game for all the bigshots.

- She was only a corset model's daughter, and she bustled by day and hustled by night.

- She was only an elevator operator's daughter, and people went down on her every day.

- She was only a carpenter's daughter, and she often got nailed and screwed.

- She was only an X-ray technician's daughter, and she often got ultraviolated.

- She was only a computer programmer's daughter, and she was a piece of user-friendly software who grabbed men's joysticks, turned their floppies into hard drives, went down at the touch of a button, was easy to enter, and let them come interface.

# The
# Bedding
# Night

Have you heard about the inexperienced bride on her wedding night? She didn't know which way to turn. First they tried it doggy style: he sat up and begged, and she rolled over and played dead. They finally ended up doing it coyote style. He prowled around the hole all night and howled.

In the loose canon of dirty wordplay, many a joke fires away at the bride and groom's first adventure in bed, a momentous event that has been defined as "the tail end of a wedding."

## Stymied

In the honeymoon suite of a plush hotel, a new bride and groom eagerly jump into the heart-shaped bed to make love together for the first time. After a wild and passionate three hours, they both reach the climactic moment simultaneously, slipping into a state of utmost relaxation. At this point the groom reaches for the telephone.

"What on earth do you think you're doing?" asks the bride.

"I wanted everything to be perfect, so I thought I should call room service for a bottle of their finest champagne," comes the reply.

"Well, I used to date Tiger Woods, and when Tiger and I finished making love, we would wait ten minutes and make love again," the groom is informed.

"If that's what you are used to, I shall gladly comply." About ten minutes later the couple is again in the throes of passionate ecstasy. At the culmination of the second whoopie session, the groom reaches for the phone once again.

"Now what do you think you're doing?" the bride inquires.

"Like I said before, this is a very special occasion, so I'm calling room service for a bottle of the bubbly."

"Well, when I was dating Tiger, we'd relax for fifteen minutes or so and then make love a third time."

So, once again, not wanting to disappoint his bride, the groom relaxes a bit and forces himself to engage in a third session of whoopie. After the climax of their climax, he once again reaches for the telephone.

"What are you doing now?" asks the bride.

"I'm calling Tiger Woods to find out what's par for this hole."


## Motherly Advice

A newly married husband and wife take over the apartment of the bride's parents and stay there on the wedding night. Before long, the mother is awakened by a loud pounding on her door. Half-asleep, she staggers to the door only to be confronted by her daughter, who is totally inexperienced in the ways of love. "Momma, momma, what do I do up there?"

The mother replies, "Don't worry, girl, just you lie back and enjoy yourself."

So the girl returns to her husband, but within a few minutes she runs screaming back down the stairs, "Momma, momma, oh, it's just awful. You'll never imagine. He took off his shirt, and he's got a big, hairy chest, just like a gorilla! I can't make love to him. It's disgusting!"

"Don't you worry," the mother soothes her daughter. "A big, hairy chest means that he's got a big, hairy love muscle. Go back up there and have a good time."

So back up the stairs goes the bride, but a few minutes later she again shows up at her mother's door, shocked and horrified at her husband's hypervirility. "Momma, momma, he's in his underpants, and it's terrible! He's got thick, hairy legs!"

The mother calmly replies, "Don't you worry, girl. With thick, hairy legs he can better drive his love muscle. Go back up and just lie down, relax, and have a good time."

So back up she goes. As she enters the room, she sees his bare feet for the first time, and one of them is mutilated and half-missing from an accident.

Back down the stairs she dashes, screaming, "Momma, momma, oh, no! I can't bear it!"

"What's the matter now, for Pete's sake?" asks the mother.

"He's got a foot and a half!"

The mother pushes the girl aside and charges up the stairs, yelling, "Out of my way, girl! You stay here! This is a job for your momma!"

## Game Plan

Frank is about to be married and goes to his friend to ask advice. "I'm a virgin, Charlie, and I have no idea what to do with Mary on our wedding night."

"It's simple," the experienced Charlie expostulates. "Go to the bedroom with Mary. You'll undress. She'll undress. She'll lie on the bed. You'll lie next to her. You'll get on top of her, and then you'll kiss her on her belly button and say, 'I love you.' After that, let nature take its course, and you'll have a great time."

On the night after the wedding, Frank follows Charlie's instructions scrupulously. He goes to bed with Mary, lies next to her, climbs on top, kisses her belly button, and says, "I love you."

Suddenly, Mary begins writhing and panting, "More! More!"

Completely confused, Frank shouts, "I love you—I love you!" faster and faster.

"Lower! lower!" Mary screams.

"I love you. I love you," says Frank, trying to get his voice down an octave lower.

## Cross-Dressing

The newlywed couple is getting undressed for their wedding whoopie. After removing his trousers, the husband tosses them to his wife and says, "Try these on!"

"What did you say?" asks the wife.

"I said try these on!"

"Well, all right," she complies and slips into her husband's trousers. Even after tightening the belt to the last loop, they're much too big for her, of course. "I can't wear these," she complains.

"You're absolutely right that you can't," crows the husband. "Now you just remember that I'm the one who will wear the pants in this family."

Right then the wife tosses the husband her panties. "Put those on!" she commands.

"What are you talking about?"

"Put them on! You made me try yours. Now you try mine!"

"All right," the husband sighs and struggles to climb into the panties, but he can't get them up past his thighs. "I can't get into these," he says.

"That's right," ripostes the bride, "and you won't get into them until you change your attitude!"

## Ups and Downs

The morning after the honeymoon night in a local hotel the bride's closest girlfriend telephones her asking how married life agrees with her.

"Oh, Gloria," the bride responds. "I'm just dead tired. All night long it was stop and start, up and down, in and out; stop and start, up and down, in and out! Don't ever take a room next to an elevator!"

## Well, Do You?

A new bride and groom make love for the first time. Relaxing afterward, the husband asks his wife, "Do you smoke after sex?"

"I don't know, dear. Until now I was a virgin," she answers. Then she looks under the covers to find the answer to her husband's question.

## All Ready

SHE: "Oh look—the bridesmaid!"
HE: "My gosh, so soon?"

"Do you smoke after sex?"

## Dis-ease

A new bride and groom who have never made love together settle down in the honeymoon suite. She is quite hot to trot, but he seems hesitant.

Slowly he takes off his shoes and socks, and the wife notices that his toes are mangled and deformed. "What happened to you?" she asks.

"When I was a little boy, I contracted tolio."

Next he removes his trousers, and the new bride sees that his knees are pockmarked and scarred. "What's going on here? What happened to your knees?"

"When I was a little boy, I contracted a bad case of kneesles."

The bride's eyes continue to travel up his body. When they come to his crotch, she smirks, "Don't tell me. When you were a little boy, you also caught smallcox!"

# Poonerisms

Perhaps you know somebody—and that somebody may be you—who occasionally says *revelant* for *relevant, aminal* for *animal, emeny* for *enemy, renumeration* for *remuneration,* and *pascetti* for *spaghetti.* Each of these mispronunciations illustrates a tendency to anticipate and, hence, to switch sounds within a word or between words.

When the effect of such a transposition becomes comic, we call the result a spoonerism, named after the Rev. William Archibald Spooner (1844–1930). Spooner was a kindly man with white hair and a cherubic face who taught at New College, Oxford, for a half century. He became so renowned for his hilarious tips of the slung—no, make that slips of the tongue—that he entered the immortal company of the Earl of Sandwich, Etienne de Silhouette, Amelia Jenks Bloomer, and others whose names have become enshrined in our vocabulary.

William Archibald Spooner admitted to "occasional infelicities in verbal diction." In church one day he is said to have said,

"Mardon me padam, you are occupewing my pie. May I sew you to another sheet?" On another occasion, he is supposed to have reprimanded a student with, "You have hissed all my mystery lectures. You have tasted a whole worm. Please leave Oxford on the next town drain!"

Lost in the mists of history is the fact that the Rev. Spooner had a younger brother, the Irrev. Peter Dick Pooner. Like Spooner, Pooner was afflicted with a bizarre penchant for reversing syllables, but, unlike his more famous brother, his always turned out to be dirty. In the field of inadvertently filthy reversals he was a clitiful putz who always wed the lay. *The Shaming of the True* and *Lacenic and Old Arse* were his favorite shit hose, and he reveled in the stories contained in *The Screwing of the Tern, The Hell-Tail Tart, French the Lieutenant's Woman, A Hard Man Is Good to Find, The Cave of the Bare Clan, Even Blowgirls Get the Cues, Body's Brown John, Bigger Knocker Tales, The Strumpet of the Wan, Tales of Rabbit Peter*, and *A Sale of Two Titties* (the story of two breast implants, as told by Darles Chickens).

Dr. Pooner shamefully moved his vowels and had a lot of wrubble with his turds, which constantly deperped his fetus and caused his ships to be slowing. On one occasion, he began a story with the sentence, "Once upon a girl there was a time." On another, he complimented his students on being "pretty fart smellers," which elicited rumorous nipples of laughter. That was astute cunt and a cold ball if there ever was one, and he was tit to be fied. No matter how much the stool formed, it was like trying to get stud from a blown. With Pooner's line fuck, it was enough to goose his cook and bare two tits his reputation. People started telling stories about his whiz and witdom, and ever since it's been the case of the tale dogging the wag.

At a dinner party, Pooner, with much thud and blunder, lifted a toast to "our queer old dean, Rictoria Vagina." On another occasion he raised his tankard to "the Deck and Dootchess of Kunt."

Pooner was not vorely sexed about his verbal disability and strove to be the faster of his mate. He always more in bind that "the best planned lays of mess and mine oft go astray" and "a turd in the hand is worth boo in the bush"—or should that be "a herd in the band is worth boo in the tush," or "A hand on the bush is worth two on the bird"?

Dr. Pooner was a farty hello who became webitched by a wordy stench from Fellows Balls, Vermont. She was a bare and fucksome gritty pearl, and soon, after the happiness of pursuit, he asked for her hole in handy matrimony. After he was titted for a fucks, they were jawfully loined amidst the peal of bedding wells. That night found that, as a couple, they were a fight tit.

In 1902 Dr. Pooner, not being an any panty husband, purchased two pickets to Tittsburgh, Sense'll Pain Ya. At dinner one night with the captain, he exclaimed, "It's my ducky lay when they serve chancy fuck, a late groin of pork, and a whore's bed at the same meal!" After the repast he is said to have had a ball-gladder attack, run to the soil it teat, and shaken an enormous tit.

Dr. and Mrs. Pooner found their whack to the balls as they sailed through fog as thick as sea poop. When the ship encountered a stormy ass of mare that made everybody feel like a dick suck, they sent out an SOS in coarse mode. The vessel shit holes trying to arrive before the short putz, but finally the Pooners landed and shopped a whore. Leaving no stern untoned, they rang the bordels of all the shitty props and with the help of a lank bone, they purchased everything to seat their nudes—a banned hag, a cool tit, some Breast to crush with, a Hell and Bowel telephone with a ball cocks, a gland hider, a crotch that they both waved, some delicious cock randy, an overdead whore for their garage—all sorts of farty acts.

The Irrev. Pooner is best remembered for *A Poonerized Dictionary*, which he compiled throughout the years of his long life. Among the most infamous of his flip entries are:

- *alimony*. Bounty on the mutiny.
- *bordello*. A toll cookie-house.
- *brassiere*. A bustblocker.
- *call girls*. The lays of our dives.
- *congressional prostitute*. A House whore.
- *erotica for police*. Cop porn.
- *fartist*. A breakwinder.
- *frigid female golf pro*. An unpliable lay.
- *frustration*. The first time that you find out you can't do it the second time.
- *utter frustration*. The second time you find out you can't do it the first time.
- *hairy breasts*. The hirsute of pappiness.
- *intercourse*. A hot pole in a pothole.
- *lousy embrace*. Bum hug.
- *male chauvinist pigs*. The misters of Circe.
- *masturbate*. Press the Meat.
- *masturbation*. Working your bone to the fingers.
- *masturbation manual*. Fifty Ways to Love Your Lever.
- *mooning*. An ass in the pane.
- *motivator*. A pyrocracktor; one who lights a fire under other people's asses.
- *necrophilia*. An act offensive to any body—to lay the ceased.
- *needlework for a bra*. Tat for tit.
- *nymphomaniac*. A woman worn out of bedlock.
- *nymphomaniacal rug-maker*. A had matter.
- *oral sex*. Something you need like a head in the hole.
- *phallus-shaped ice-cream cup*. A porn cone.

- *poker prostitute*. A hardcore card whore.

- *porn actor*. A man whose rise is starring.

- *porn actress*. A woman who puts the heart before the coarse.

- *pricing for a silicone treatment*. A titbid.

- *prostitute*. A walkahoric. One for whom it's a business doing pleasure with her customers.

- *sex organs*. Meat to please you.

- *sickly erection*. A perpendicular dick-en-purpler.

- *whorehouse*. A nymph lode.

The bass ackwards Pooner may have departed the earthly stage decades ago, but the spirit of his salacious transpositions lives on in many forms:

## Heard You Have?

- Have you heard about the midget who was fired from the circus?
  *He was sticking his nose in everybody's business.*

- Have you heard about the tall man who was fired from the circus?
  *He was sticking his business in everybody's nose.*

- Have you heard about the man who went to buy a seersucker at Cox's but ended up, instead, at Sears?

- Have you heard about the four McCoy brothers?
  *The first worked in a factory as a sock tucker. The second worked in a factory as a cork soaker. The third worked in a factory as a coke sacker. And the fourth brother—he was the real McCoy.*

- Have you heard about the man who spilled clam chowder on his trousers?
  *He complained, "Waiter, there's soup in my fly!"*

- Have you heard about the fabulous stripteaser?
  *As the crowd watches, she wowed crotches.*

- Have you heard about the German spy who was eager to become a wife?
  *Her name was Hotta Marry.*

- Have you heard about the football coach whose penis was so big that the weight caused his legs to buckle?
  *His name was Root Knock-knee.*

- Have you heard about the elderly sadomasochist?
  *His name was Whip van Wrinkle.*

- Have you heard about the aggressive prostitute?
  *Her name was Pole Courter.*

- Have you heard about the busty old lady?
  *Her name was Elder Cleavage.*

- Have you heard about Bonnie Parker?
  *She was a barren robber.*

- Have you heard about the new government program that gives money to women with big tits?
  *It's called the bust dole.*

- Have you heard about the confused dairy farmer?
  *He kept gripping his steers.*

- Have you heard about the organization dedicated to preserving wooden toilets?
  *It's called the Birch John Society.*

- Have you heard about the cannibalistic nurse?
  *First, she'd prick your boil . . .*

- Have you heard about the woman who became a devotee of a swami and fell in love with the man?
  *She studied at the meat of her faster.*

## Pooneristic Quickies

- What did the first-grade teacher say to her pupils about getting in line to go to the bathroom?
"Watch your queues and pee."

- What did the doctor say after he made a house call to the bordello?
*"Whore is well."*

- What do you call it when Constance says, "Suck my tits, Mellors" and "Fuck me, Mellors"?
*Lady Loverley's Chatter.*

- Why do people enjoy telling jokes about shit?
*Because mess is lore.*

- What did the cannibal give his wife for her birthday?
*A box of Farmer's Fannies.*

- How do you titillate an ocelot?
*You oscillate its tit a lot.*

- It's colder than a teacher's wit!

- Remember: It's better to finger your prick than to prick your finger. It's better to park your meat in a woman than to meet your woman in a park.
And it's not how long you make it, but how you make it long.

- In spite of their parents' fulminations about the evils of masturbation, the boys soon had wangs tugging.

- When you step in sheep dip, you are in deep shit.

- It isn't any Joe Blob who can get a blow job.

- British statesman Sir Stafford Cripps had a name that seemed to invite others to poonerize it as Sir Stifford Crapps—and they often did.

It isn't any Joe Blob who can get a blow job.

- Radio blooper: "Good evening, ladies and gentlemen, and welcome to another series of classical music programs on the Canadian Broadcorping Castration."

- Announcement at a concert: "Miss Playbody will pee for us."

- Birth control slogan: "Accidents Cause People."

- Only the young die good.

- HE: "I'll fuck you, so help me!"
  SHE: "I'll help you, so fuck me!"

- What movie starring Tom Hanks tells the story of how a urologist cures a famous fastball pitcher from Texas after a line drive hits him in the crotch?
  *Saving Ryan's Privates.*

- Have you heard about the rabbit who just washed her thing and couldn't do a hare with it?

- Some nurses can make the bed without disturbing the patient. Others make the patient without disturbing the bed.

## A Mickey Mouse Tale

It is a little-known fact that in 1958 Mickey Mouse took Minnie Mouse to court to file for divorce. When the judge asked the All-American rodent why, after so many years of wedded bliss, he wished to end the marriage, Mickey replied: "She's fucking Goofy! And that's not all. Minnie has been banging the other animated characters all over town. She'll strip for any comic strip star that comes along!

"She's been Scrooged by McDuck, peckered by Woody, and buggered by Bugs! You want to know what's green and smells like a rat's crotch? The answer is Kermit the Frog's face. I know because he's been hopping my wife for years! She's also been sitting on that nosy splinterhead Pinocchio's face, and you know what she says to him? 'Lie to me, Pinocchio, lie! Now tell the truth! Now lie to me! Now tell the truth!' "

How did Mickey uncover all this dirt? Because he found a secret journal that Minnie kept over the years, and he read it all. The title: *Diary of a Had Mousewife*.

## Is Chivalry Dead?

A stout elderly woman enters a room in which an elderly gentleman is sitting. When he does not rise, she chides him, "I see that you are not so gallant as when you were a boy!"

He shoots right back: "And I see that you are not so buoyant as when you were a gal!"

## Age-old Problem

An aging woman in bed with her even more aging husband turns to him and says, "I'd like to do it tonight, but I'm afraid my back might peter out."

He answers, "So would I, but I'm afraid my peter might back out."

## Can't Get the Hang of It

An instrumentalist of the sixties British band whose hit was "Wild Thing" lost his member in a freak accident. The doctor tried to fit him with a prosthesis, but the musician couldn't make it work. Lamented the doctor, "You can't teach an old Trogg new dicks."

## Fan Club

The son of a shah is called a shan. A certain shan is afflicted with epilepsy. One day the shan, moving amongst his harem, is smitten with a seizure. When his attendants arrive shortly thereafter, the harem girls inquire of them: "Where were you when the fit hit the shan?"

## Getting to the Bottom of Things

Benny has a most embarrassing problem. Whenever he farts, the wind makes the sound "Honda!"

Reasoning that the Japanese know the most about Hondas, Benny desperately seeks the help of a Japanese proctologist. "Why," asks Benny, "does my passing gas make the sound 'Honda'?"

The proctologist probes the man's anal passage and discovers therein a pustule. "Aha!" exults the doctor. "I have found the source of your problem. Abscess make the fart go Honda!"

## Bring On the Clones

A famous biologist takes to the lecture circuit and soon finds that the grind of speaking appearances makes it impossible for him to pursue his research and practice. To solve the dilemma, he creates a clone of himself and sends the reproduction on the lecture tour, so that he, the original doctor, can pursue his studies.

Although the clone looks exactly like the doctor, he possesses one tragic flaw: the clone has a compulsion to utter dirty words in incredible profusion, and soon he ruins the doctor's reputation.

Enraged, the doctor summons the clone to his penthouse apartment and explains that the experiment is a failure and that the clone's life will have to be terminated.

"You can't do that!" protests the clone. "I'm a living human being!"

"No, you're not," counters the doctor. "I made you, and I can destroy you."

The two of them—doctor and clone—get into a fierce shoving match, and in the melee, the clone falls backwards, shatters the picture window, and splatters on the pavement far below.

The police come and question the doctor, who explains what has happened. The cops then charge the doctor with making an obscene clone fall.

## Rocking the Boat

Four men on a trip through the Canadian wilderness telegraph, "Need four punts and a canoe at once." The answer arrives: "Women on the way, but what the hell's a panoe?"

## Mass Confusion

The newly ordained priest at his first mass is so frightened that he barely bumbles through the sermon. Before his second week at the pulpit he asks the monsignor what he can do to relax. The older man answers, "Next week it might help if you put some martinis into your pitcher of water."

On the Sunday of that second week, the young priest talks up a storm. After his hour-long sermon, he asks the monsignor, "How did I do?"

"Fine," replies the monsignor, "but there are a few things you should remember before you address the congregation again.

"Next time, *sip* your martini rather than gulp it down glassful after glassful.

"There are ten commandments, not twelve.

"There are twelve disciples, not ten.

"David slew Goliath; he did not kick the shit out of him.

"It's the Virgin Mary, not Mary with the cherry.

"We do not refer to the Savior and his disciples as J.C. and the boys.

"And last but not least, next Sunday there will be a taffy-pulling contest at St. Peter's, not a peter-pulling contest at St. Taffy's!"

## Bird Turd

A hunter is out shooting game in the wilds of Africa. When he comes to a certain part of the jungle, all of his native bearers bolt in panic, save one—his most faithful companion.

When the hunter asks the remaining bearer why the others have fled and what the hell is going on, he replies, "You are about to enter the territory of the Great and Terrible Foo Bird. The Foo Bird has sixty-four teeth and a hundred-foot wingspan, but the most terrible thing about him is that, if you step on his turf, he will fly over you and shit on your head, and if you wipe it off, you die!"

"Balderdash!" sneers the hunter, and takes another step. Immediately the sky darkens as the Great and Terrible Foo Bird swoops down and plants a humongous turd on the hunter's head.

Afraid to wipe off the Foo Bird pat that now sits upon his scalp, the hunter lives with it for five endless years. But it stinks horribly and has an incredibly long half-life. Finally, the hunter can't stand the stench and social isolation any longer. He wipes off the turd.

And his head falls off and he dies.

IMMORAL: If the Foo shits, wear it.

# What's the Difference?

Many English-speaking children cut their punning eyeteeth by hearing and posing a special kind of riddle. Each question begins with the formula "What's the difference between . . . ?" and the answer is often in the form of a spoonerism:

- What's the difference between a mouse and a pretty girl?
  *One harms the cheese; the other charms the he's.*

- What's the difference between a tube and a crazy Dutchman?
  *One is a hollow cylinder; the other is a silly Hollander.*

When those children grow older, they often graduate to a pooneristic version of the old riddles. Try this one:

- What's the difference between a cleverly poonerized pun and a fart?
  *A cleverly poonerized pun is a shaft of wit.*

Part of the delight of these question-and-answer jokes is that the jokester doesn't have to utter a single dirty word in the answer, as witness these classics:

- What's the difference between a rooster and a lawyer?
  *A rooster clucks defiance.*

- What's the difference between an epileptic oysterman and a whore with diarrhea?
  *An epileptic oysterman shucks between fits.*

- What's the difference between a magician and the Rockettes chorus line?
  *A magician has a cunning array of stunts.*

- What's the difference between a noisemaker and a flatulent road worker?
  *A noisemaker is a party favor.*

- What's the difference between a poor marksman and a constipated owl?
  *A poor marksman shoots but never hits.*

- What's the difference between a nun at vespers and a nun in the bathtub?
  *A nun at vespers has hope in her soul.*

- What's the difference between a feathered-hat maker and a good lay?
  *A feathered-hat maker is a pheasant plucker.*

- What's the difference between a football game and the Oscar for best actress?
  *In a football game they kick a punt.*

- What's the difference between a razor factory in England and what a stacked woman is built like?
  *A razor factory in England is a Brit Schickhouse.*

- What's the difference between a pickpocket and a Peeping Tom?
  *A pickpocket snatches watches.*

- What's the difference between a racing vehicle and a porn-film actor?
  *A racing vehicle is a stock car.*

- What's the difference between a year-round skier and wasp semen?
  *A year-round skier is a ski bum.*

- What's the difference between an identical female sibling and a tornado in a whorehouse?
  *An identical female sibling is a twin sister.*

- What's the difference between a fox chase and Lady Godiva?
  *A fox chase is a hunt on a course.*

- What's the difference between a religious cultist and a fat whore?
  *A religious cultist is a holy roller.*

- What's the difference between a hunting dog and a nympho-maniac?
  *A hunting dog sics a duck.*

- What's the difference between a stout woman and a virgin?
  *A stout woman is trying to diet.*

- What's the difference between an oversupply of oil and a spry whore?
  *An oversupply of oil is the same old glut.*

- What's the difference between a baby boy and an opera director?
  *A baby boy sucks his fingers.*

- What's the difference between a cattle stampede and a line of bathing beauties?
  *A cattle stampede is a bunch of running steers.*

- What's the difference between a nearby landfill and a great lay?
  *A nearby landfill is a handy dump.*

- What's the difference between the Panama Canal and an airhead?
  *One is a busy ditch.*

- What's the difference between a fish and a horny bear?
  *A fish mucks around a fountain.*

- What's the difference between a horny sheath on a toe and an unsuccessful date?
  *A horny sheath on a toe is a toenail.*

- What's the difference between an expired hillbilly and someone you can't stand?
  *An expired hillbilly is a hick dead.*

- What's the difference between a thief and a pimp?
  *A thief is a purse snatcher.*

- What's the difference between a counterfeit dollar and a skinny lady?
  *A counterfeit dollar is a phony buck.*

- What's the difference between a big crack in the street and an erection?
  *A big crack in the street is a pothole.*

- What's the difference between a case of liquor and a female hockey team?
  *A case of liquor is a crating of scotch.*

- What's the difference between discordant sound and artificial excrement?
  *One is cacophony.*

- What's the difference between nostalgia for an old piece of music and a piece of ass?
  *One is tune pang.*

- What's the difference between a complex musical composition and an oversexed woman?
  *A complex musical composition is a symphony, and an oversexed woman is a nympho (see?).*
- What's the difference between a Ritz cracker and one who eats pussy?
  *One's a snack cracker.*
- What's the difference between a third-base coach and a sexually active bachelor?
  *The third-base coach calls the bunts.*
- What's the difference between a seagull and a puppy?
  *A seagull flits across the shore.*
- What's the difference between a young man and an old man?
  *A young man has wet dreams and dry farts.*
- What's the difference between a student and a pimp?
  *A student cracks books.*
- What's the difference between a bull and Lawrence Welk's band?
  *On a bull the horns are in the front and the asshole is in the back.*

"What's the difference . . ." jokes are so versatile that they can appear in many forms other than poonerisms:

- What's the difference between a lightbulb and a pregnant woman?
  *You can always unscrew a lightbulb.*
- What's the difference between a bonus and a penis?
  *A woman will always blow a man's bonus.*
- What's the difference between a mind and an ass?
  *A woman will always give you a piece of her mind.*
- What's the difference between "dark" and "hard"?
  *It gets dark every night.*
- What's the difference between parsley and pussy?
  *Nobody eats parsley.*

- What's the difference between a brownnoser and a shithead? *Depth perception.*

- What's the difference between a genealogist and a gynecologist?
  *A genealogist looks up the family tree, while a gynecologist looks up the family bush.*

- What's the difference between a new job and a new bride?
  *After six months, the new job still sucks.*

- What's the difference between herpes and marriage?
  *Herpes lasts forever.*

- What's the difference between a rooster and a nymphomaniac?
  *A rooster says, "Cockadoodledoo." A nympho says, "Any cock'll do."*

- What's the difference between a sewing machine and a female jogger?
  *A sewing machine has only one bobbin.*

- What's the difference between Ex-Lax and Sex-Lax?
  *Ex-Lax is for people who have trouble going.*

- What's the difference between a Big Mac and a blow job?
  *You don't know? How about lunch tomorrow?*

- What's the difference between a snowman and a snow woman?
  *Snowballs.*

- What's the difference between male and female pancakes?
  *Female pancakes are stacked.*

- What's the difference between a male and a female chromosome?
  *If you want to find out, pull down its genes.*

- What's the difference between a café and a stacked woman?
  *One is a barroom, and the other is barooooom!*

What's the difference between a snowman
and a snow woman?

- What's the difference between a used tire and 365 used condoms?
  *One is a Goodyear, and the other is a great year!*

- What's the difference between your fish and your meat?
  *If you beat your fish, it dies.*

- What's the difference between light and hard?
  *You can sleep with a light on.*

- What's the difference between a pig and a fox?
  *About three drinks.*

- What's the difference between a Lifesaver and a man?
  *A Lifesaver comes in five flavors.*

- What's the difference between quiche and pussy?
  *Real men don't eat quiche.*

- What's the difference between a Mercedes and a nymphomaniac?
  *Some people have never been in a Mercedes.*

- What's the difference between boiled water and pea soup?
  *Anyone can boil water.*

- What's the difference between a porcupine and a tourist bus?
  *A porcupine has the pricks on the outside.*

- What's the difference between spectacles and a woman?
  *Spectacles sit higher up on your face.*

- What's the difference between a prompt airline and a man with ten children?
  *A prompt airline always pulls out on time.*

- What's the difference between a one-lane country road and 69?
  *On a one-lane country highway you can see the asshole in front of you.*

- What's the difference between a prude and a prune?
  *Nothing; they both have a long shelf life.*

- What's the difference between a snake and a goose?
  *A snake is an asp in the grass, and a goose is a clasp in the ass.*

- What's the difference between a long-legged bird and a hot pussy?
  *A long-legged bird is a flamingo, and a hot pussy is a flaming o.*

- What's the difference between towels and toilet paper?
  *You don't know? Then don't come to my house.*

- What's the difference between a fish and an excited woman?
  *When a fish wiggles its tail, it's going.*

- What's the difference between war and peace?
  *There has never been a good war.*

- What's the difference between an enzyme and a hormone?
  *You can't hear an enzyme.*

- What's the difference between medium and rare?
  *Six inches is medium. Eight inches is rare.*

- What's the difference between a boxer and a woman?
  *A boxer stands up to get knocked down, and a woman lies down to get knocked up.*

- What's the difference between a lawyer and a gigolo?
  *A gigolo only screws one person at a time.*

- What's the difference between a chicken and a baby?
  *A chicken is the result of a sitting hen while the baby is the result of a standing cock.*

- What's the difference between a condom and a coffin?
  *You come in one and go in the other.*

- What's the difference between purple and pink?
  *The grip.*

- What's the difference between a penis and a prick?
  *A penis is fun, sexy, and satisfying. A prick is the guy who owns it.*

- What's the difference between a big cat and a little cat?
  *A big cat will scratch and bite, but a little pussy never hurt any-body.*

- What's the difference between sin and shame?
  *It is a sin to put it in, but it's a shame to pull it out.*

- What's the difference between a sorority girl and a bowling ball?
  *You can only put three fingers in a bowling ball.*

- What's the difference between a divorce and a circumcision?
  *With a divorce, you get rid of the whole prick.*

- What's the difference between oral sex and anal sex?
  *Oral sex makes your whole day; anal sex makes your hole weak.*

# Slinging
# Muddle

Circus showman P. T. Barnum once had a problem of over-crowding in his popular New York wild animal museum. Patrons were so enchanted by the lions, snakes, and other creatures that they were apt to stay too long, thus preventing new customers from joining the throng.

Barnum solved his problem by taking down the EXIT sign over the doorway to the street and replacing it with a sign that said TO THE EGRESS. Thinking that some kind of exotic bird, like an egret, was flapping behind the door, members of the crowd stepped through—and found themselves out on the street.

Barnum's clever strategy illustrates how beguiling and misleading big, high-sounding words can be when we don't quite grasp their meanings.

The 1950 Florida Democratic primary for the Senate pitted incumbent Claude Pepper against then-Congressman George Smathers. The following is an expansion of a statement that,

223

according to political folklore, appeared in unsigned pamphlets or in actual stumping orations that Smathers trotted around the North Florida pinelands.

Pepper lost the race, but went on to a long and distinguished service in the House. Smathers retired from the Senate in 1971, vigorously denying responsibility until the end. Thirty years after the primary, the *New York Times* said it confirmed his claim, but Smathers acknowledged that the tale has by now "gone into the history books." Whether apocryphal or not, the basic concept provides a lively example of how you can sling muddle at your opponents and not get taken to court—and how pornography is, simply, in the crotch of the beholder.

"My fellow citizens, it is my patriotic duty to inform you of some disturbing facts about my opponent.

"Are you aware of the fact that the Senator is a known sexagenarian? He is a flagrant Homo sapiens who for years has been practicing celibacy all by himself. He has been seen on repeated occasions masticating in public restaurants, and he even vacillated once on the Senate Floor!

"In fact, your senator is a confessed heterosexual who advocates and even participates in social intercourse in mixed company.

"He habitually visits the YMCA, where he frequently engages in abdominal exercises, while at the golf course he perpetrates horrible lies.

"His very home is a den of propinquity. The place is suffused with an atmosphere of incense, and there, in the privacy of his own residence, he practices nepotism and extroversion with members of his own family.

"Now let's take a close look at the salubrious acts committed by the members of the Senator's family:

"It is a controvertible fact that his father, who died of a degenerative disease, made his money publishing phonographic magazines and distributing pamphlets about horticulture.

"His mother was a known equestrienne who nourished colts

He has been seen on repeated occasions
masticating in public restaurants. . . .

on her country estate and practiced her diversions out in the field.

"His daughter, who is powerfully attracted to sects, is a well-known proselyte, who accosts lay people outside of churches.

"Not surprisingly another daughter pursues a hortative life and offers advice filled with hoary platitudes.

"His son matriculates openly at Harvard University and is a member of an all-male sextet.

"For many years his sister was employed as a floor-walker, and she practiced her calling in some of our city's best department stores.

"His brother was known to consort with numismatists and philatelists and spent three years living in a Buddhist colony.

"His uncle, a purveyor of used condominiums, goes to movies almost every night and has turned into a heroine addict.

"His aunt is so susceptible to moral suasion that she has been pushing for oral hygiene in our schools.

"And at this very moment the Senator's wife is off in wicked New York City living the life of a thespian and performing her histrionic acts before paying customers!

"Now I ask you. Do you want a man with such an explicable and veracious reputation occupying public office and setting an example for our youth, who under his influence might convert to altruism?

"Clearly a vote for my opponent is a vote for the perpetuation of all we hold dear. A vote for me is a vote for the very antithesis of the American way."

# Euphemistic Cussing

*Banish the use of those four-letter words*
 *Whose meanings are never obscure.*
*The Anglos, the Saxons, those bawdy old birds,*
 *Were vulgar, obscene, and impure.*
*But cherish the use of the weaseling phrase*
 *That never quite says what it means.*
*You'd better be known for your hypocrite ways*
 *Than be vulgar, impure, and obscene.*

A British civil servant was filling out a government job application when he came to a section of the form that asked, "Parents: alive or deceased? If deceased, please explain circumstances." The man broke into a sweat, for his father had recently been hanged as a criminal. Fearing that he would not get the job, the applicant wrote in the blank, "My father was attending a public ceremony when the platform gave way."

This bit of gallows humor is a choice example of a euphemism

(Greek: *eu*, "good"; *pheme*, "speech"), an attempt to use an indirect, favorable word or expression in place of something more direct and harsh. A euphemism calls a spade a heart and tells it like it isn't, in other words.

Americans have pressed into service a special kind of word-mincing called taboo euphemisms to maneuver through and around matters of religion, sex, and body functions. Who needs to shout "hell!" when Sam Hill ("damn hell") is available to help us cuss (a softening of "curse") euphemistically? Sam Hill was not a particular person, and Sam Hill expressions such as "what the Sam Hill" and "mad as Sam Hill" originated in the American West and were first captured in print in 1839. Sam Hill was exceedingly popular with frontiersmen, especially when they needed to clean up their language in the presence of womenfolk. Additional softenings of "hell" include *heck, hey, Halifax, Hoboken,* and *Jesse* ("If you don't watch out, you are going to catch Jesse.").

We enlist battalions of taboo euphemisms to help us tiptoe around religious terms. It's a strange world in which calling out the name of Jesus Christ in church is a sign of moral rectitude, but, once outside, we have to find ways of not pronouncing those words. Socially acceptable ways of expressing "Jesus Christ!" include *Judas Priest, gee, gee whiz* (which sounds like "Je-sus"), *gee whillikers, Christmas, jesum crow, holy cow, holy crow, cripes, criminey, by Jingo, by Jiminy, Jiminy Crickets, Jiminy Christmas,* and even *jeepers creepers.*

Closely related are the ways we avoid saying "God" and "damnation," most of these devices having originated in the seventeenth and eighteenth centuries: *gosh, goodness gracious, good grief, good gravy, gar, golly, gol dang, doggone, by gum, dad gum, drat it* ("God rot it"), *dear me* (a phonetic variation of the Italian *Dio mio,* "my God"), *jumpin' Jehoshaphat* ("jumpin' Jehovah"), *begorrah, great Scott, by Godfrey, by gorey,* and W. C. Fields's *Godfrey Daniels.* Older and more elegant stratagems for skirting the name "God" are *egad* ("ye gods"), *odds bodkins* (a shortening of "God's body"), *gadzooks* ("God's hooks": the nails of the cross), *'Sblood* ("God's blood"), and *zounds* ("by God's wounds").

The biblical commandment not to take the Lord's name in vain and Christ's injunction to eschew all swearing, either by heaven or by earth, have affected all areas of dirty talk. Just as *gee whiz* and *gosh* elide the names of Jesus Christ and God, *shucks, shoot, sugar, shaving cream, spit, fudge, frig, futz around, freaking, stuffed* (British), *bug off, butt* (for "buttocks"), *bazooms* ("bosoms"), and *schmo* ("schmuck") retain just enough key consonants and vowels to make clear their references to certain other taboo words. As comedian George Carlin has observed, "*Shoot* is simply *shit* with two *o*'s."

Hugh Rawson in his *Dictionary of Euphemisms and Other Doubletalk* (Crown, 1981) recounts the strange history of *arse*: "One of the first indications of the new niceness of the eighteenth century is the taint that was attached to 'ass' after it became a euphemism for *arse* (the real term is now used cutely but quite mistakenly as a euphemism for the euphemism!). As early as 1751, polite ladies, whose equally polite grandmothers had thought it clever to say "arse," were shying clear of "ass" no matter what the occasion, with the result that a new euphemistic name had to be devised for the four-legged kind; hence, the appearance of *donkey*."

Euphemistic fig leaves come in all sorts of forms—and that's no bull, which is clearly a clipping of a more offensive compound, in rather the same manner that *horsefeathers* is a fastidious version of another. *Ticked off* and *take a whiz* sanitize "pissed off" and "take a piss." If such approximations are too revealing, one can always resort to acronyms (*snafu* does *not* stand for "situation normal, all *fouled* up") or initialisms, such as *BS, TS, BO, PO'd, BM, VD, B and D*, and *S/M*, the last two sounding less painful than "bondage and discipline" and "sadomasochism." When we talk about people sleeping with each other, we aren't really referring to the activity of sleep, and in the course of a one-night stand, who's standing?

Human beings apparently believe that a stinkweed by any other name will smell like a rose. The abundant resourcefulness employed in the service of mincing cusswords shows how ingenious we can be about cursing and getting away with it.

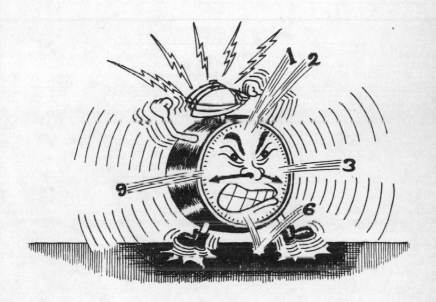

Ticked off

# Two
# Taboo-Boo
# Words

*To gain the language,*
*'Tis needful that the most immodest word*
*Be looked upon and learn'd,*

proclaimed Falstaff in Shakespeare's *Henry IV, Part II.*

Centuries later, Walt Whitman called for a "Real Dictionary" that would include and discuss "the bad words [of] unhemmed latitude, coarseness, directness, live epithets, expletives, words of opprobrium."

Following the leads of England's and America's most exuberant poets, let's have a look at one of the most direct and colorful words in the English language, namely *fuck*. This magical word can, just by its sound, describe pain and pleasure, joy and frustration, hate and love.

In popular etymology, *fuck* descends from the acronym "For Unlawful Carnal Knowledge" and was used as a form of convenient shorthand for recording cases of rape and sodomy. The leading candidate for legitimate ancestry is the German word *fokken,* meaning "to breed cattle" or "to poke, to thrust."

*Fuck* and *fucking* fall into many grammatical categories:

noun: *I don't give a fuck.*

active verb: *John fucked Mary.*

passive verb: *John was fucked in that business deal.*

adjective: *Where's my fucking shoe?*

adverb: *It's fucking cold outside.*

interjection: *Oh, fuck! I left my condoms at Mary's house.*

We English speakers are quite used to employing prefixes, as in *pre*war and *anti*war, and suffixes, as in good*ness* and fertil*ize,* but we seldom press into service infixes, word elements plunked right into the middle of another word. *Fucking,* however, holds the distinction of being the most widely used infix in the U.S. of A., as in "That's in-fucking-credible" and "It's un-fucking-believable."

It is indeed in its participial form, *fucking,* that *fuck* turns its best tricks:

A woman walks into an ice-cream parlor to order a gallon of chocolate.

"I'm sorry," says the man behind the counter, "but we're out of chocolate ice cream."

"In that case," says the customer, "I'll take some chocolate."

"I guess you didn't hear me. I said we've run out of chocolate."

"Then please give me a gallon of chocolate."

His frustration reaching the boiling point, the man asks, "Madam, will you please spell *van,* as in *vanilla?*"

"Okay. V-A-N."

."Good. Now would you please spell *straw,* as in *strawberry?*"

"S-T-R-A-W."

."And would you please spell *fuck,* as in *chocolate?*"

"What?" protests the woman. "There isn't any *fuck* in *chocolate*."

"That's exactly what I've been trying to tell you for the past fifteen minutes!"

Besides its sexual denotations and connotations, *fuck* and its variants can be used to describe many emotions and situations:

* fraud: *I got fucked by my broker.*
* dismay: *Oh, fuck it.*
* trouble: *I guess I'm fucked now.*
* aggression: *Fuck you.*
* passion: *Fuck me.*
* difficulty: *I can't figure out this fucking VCR.*
* despair: *Fucked again.*
* resignation: *I don't give a fuck.*
* incompetence: *He's a fuck-up.*
* religion: *Holy fuck!*
* laziness: *She's such a fuck-off*
* displeasure: *What the fuck's going on?*
* rebellion: *Fuck it!*

Three kinds of sex have been identified:

* *house sex:* When you're newly married and have sex all over the house in every room.
* *bedroom sex:* After you've been married for a while, you have sex just in the bedroom.
* *hall sex:* After you've been married for many, many years, you just pass each other in the hallway and say, "Fuck you!"

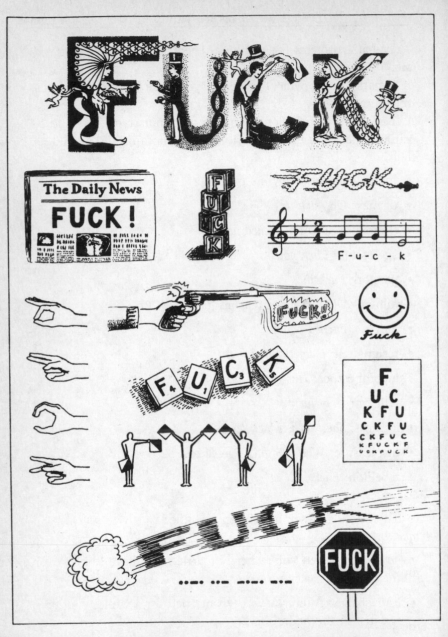

The mind boggles at the many creative forms for this
exceedingly functional word.

The mind boggles at the many creative forms for this exceedingly functional word. It can be used to enhance the meaning of almost any other word, whether that word be complimentary or pejorative: *She's so fucking beautiful; he's so fucking stupid.* Has it ever struck you as bizarre that, when you say, "Go fuck yourself!", you are expressing one of the most pleasurable acts imaginable as an insult to others?

So how can anyone be offended when you say *fuck?* Sprinkle it on your daily conversation. Tell someone to get fucked, you motherfucker.

Now let's move on to another four-letter word that outshines even *fuck* in its color, variety, and applicability. By a process of elimination you can guess that the word is *shit*, which describes a rare substance that smells worse when it is fresh than when it is stale. Those people who don't give a *shit* and who "wouldn't say shit if they had a mouthful" may be fascinated to discover the many useful and striking ways that the word is bandied about in everyday speech. No shit!

The use of *shit* embraces a wide range of human emotions, experiences, and objects. Now that it's time for me to shit or get off the pot, I'll organize the myriad manifestations of *shit* into a shitlist containing a manageable number of discrete (as well as excrete) categories. Edgar Allan Poe defined a short story as "a piece of fiction that can be read at a single sitting." This chapter is meant to be read at a single shitting.

Born from the Old English *scitan, "to defecate,"* shit continues to be used in its literal meaning—*shit pot, shit paper, shithouse, take a shit, I've got the shits,* and *Well, I'll be dipped in shit!*

In addition to its literal uses, figurative extensions of *shit* have multiplied excrementally: *up Shit Creek without a paddle, where were you when the shit hit the fan, a wish in one hand and shit in the other, built like a brick shithouse,* and *a sad sack of shit* (whence the origin of the famous GI character).

Like *fuck, shit* can be used as an all-purpose interjection—*shit! holy shit! no shit!*—or as a grammatical intensifier—*can't swim* (*run*, etc.) *for shit* (or *worth a shit*), *who the shit are you*, and *let's get the shit out of here.*

*Shit*, cojoined with animal names, means "I don't believe a word of it," as in *pig, buzzard, hen, owl, whale, dog, chicken, turtle, rat, cat,* and *bat,* as well as the ever popular *horseshit.* People go especially *apeshit* over *bullshit,* probably because of the prodigious quantity of droppings associated with the beast. I'm not *as full of shit as a Christmas turkey,* believe me, when I tell you that on payday *the eagle shits,* referring to the government symbol of the bald eagle.

Which reminds me of the story of the frog and the eagle. A frog laments aloud that nature has not granted him the ability to soar in the sky like a bird. An eagle, overhearing the amphibian's plaint, swoops down and offers the frog a ride in the sky. "Just crawl up into my asshole, and I'll take you for a spin," promises the eagle.

The frog gladly complies, and the eagle flies up and up, eventually reaching an altitude of twenty thousand feet.

At this point, the frog pokes his head out of the eagle's anal passage, looks at the ground far below, and gulps, "You wouldn't shit me, would you?"

It is, indeed, interesting to note how shit and feelings of fear are linked in our minds and speech: *scared shitless, scare the shit out of, shit green* (or *blue*), *shit bricks, shit bullets, shit little blue cookies, shit out of luck, almost shit in his pants* (or *britches*), *on his shitlist, have a shit hemorrhage, shit out of luck, I'm in deep shit.*

Speaking of being in deep shit, one classic story tells of a drunkard who stumbled into a shithouse and fell into a pit of shit. Up to his neck in the stuff, he began hollering "Fire! Fire!"

People came running, pulled him out, and cleaned him off. Then the man's rescuers asked him why he had yelled "Fire!"

"Do you think anyone would have come if I screamed 'Shit!'?" he asked.

*Shit* has added immeasurably to the art of the insult, as in *shit on you, go shit in your hat (and pull it down over your ears),* *full of shit, a crock of shit, tough shit, shit-head* (recall Lieutenant Scheisskopf in *Catch-22*), *you little shit, stupid shit, dumbshit, simple shit, dipshit, shitheel, chicken shit, lower than dogshit, he don't know shit from Shinola, that shit don't fetch, to be shit on, not worth a shit, diddly* (or *doodly*) *shit, don't know whether to shit or go blind, he thinks his shit don't stink, he thinks he's King Shit, wipe that shit-eating grin off your face,* and *eat shit!*

What two pronouns constitute fighting words? *Each, it.*

One of my favorite bumper stickers is "How's My Driving? Call 1-800-EAT-SHIT."

*Shit* can refer to almost anything, as in *who put all this shit on my bed?*

*Shit* is such a versatile word that we use it to label talk—*shoot the shit, shovel the shit, I shit you not, that's a bunch of shit;* food—*shit on a shingle* (or stick), usually referring to chipped beef or ground meat on toast and often acronymed *SOS;* human innards—*beat, kick,* or *knock the shit out of;* the human mind—*we've got to get our shit together;* drunkenness—*I got shitfaced last night;* heroin and marijuana—*that was a packet of bad shit;* and misfortune—*where were you when the shit hit the fan?* and *shit happens.*

If somebody says to you, "You don't know Jack Shit," you can riposte with:

Sure I do. Jack is the only son of Oh Shit and Awe Shit. The Shits are the owner Kneedeep & Shit Inn.

Jack Shit married Noe Shit, and they had six children—Holy, Fulla, Giva, Bull, and the twins Deep and Dip.

After a time, Dip married her drop-out high-school sweetheart Dumb, while Deep married Lotta, and they produced a daughter Loda and a nervous son Chicken.

Fulla and Giva married the Happens brothers, each becoming a Shit Happens.

Noe married one Mr. Sherlock and became known as Noe Shit Sherlock.

Bull left home to tour the world and recently returned from Italy with his new bride, Pisa Shit. They are expecting baby Shit any day.

So when somebody says, "You don't know Jack Shit," you can correct them.

Using *shit* creatively, we can even express the essence of the world's great religions and philosophies:

*Taoism:* Shit happens.

*Confucianism:* Confucius say, "Shit happens."

*Buddhism:* If shit happens, it really isn't shit.

*Zen:* What is the sound of shit happening?

*Hinduism:* This shit happened before.

*Islam:* If shit happens, it is the will of Allah, so take a hostage.

*Atheism:* I don't believe this shit.

*Agnosticism:* Maybe shit happens. Maybe it doesn't.

*Unitarianism:* I love all shit.

*Rastafarianism:* Let's smoke this shit.

*Presbyterianism:* Let shit happen to someone else.

*Calvinism:* Shit happens because you don't work hard enough.

*Episcopalianism:* If shit happens, it should not stink.

*Catholicism:* If shit happens, you deserve it.

*Christian Science:* If shit happens, don't worry. It will go away by itself.

*Moonies:* Only happy shit really happens.

*Seventh-Day Adventism:* Shit happens on Saturday.

*Jehovah's Witness:* Knock. Knock! Shit happens.

*Hare Krishna:* Shit happens, rama rama ding ding.

*Televangelism:* Send money immediately or shit will happen to you.

*Hedonism:* When shit happens, enjoy it.

*Existentialism:* What is shit, anyway?

*Stoicism:* So shit happens. Big deal. I can take it.

*Judaism:* Why does shit always happen to us?

*Nihilism:* Who gives a shit?

All of which reminds me of two questions that puzzle even the most learned of language experts:

1. What is the past tense of the verb *to shit*?
2. Why do we say that we take a shit when we actually *leave* a shit?

# A Swift
# Seduction

During the early part of this century, boys and girls grew up devouring fourteen million copies of the adventures of Tom Swift. Tom was a sterling young hero who survived one harrowing experience after another while inventing everything from the motorcycle to the fax machine, an electric airplane to a wizard camera.

In the course of the heroic action, Tom and his friends and enemies never just said something: they always said it *excitedly* or *sadly* or *hurriedly,* and in the sixties the novels inspired an entire genre of jokes, known as Tom Swifties, parodying the literary style of the Tom Swift tales:

- "I lost my flower," said Tom lackadaisically.
- "I love reading *Moby-Dick*," said Tom superficially.
- "My pet frog died," Tom croaked.
- "I used to be a pilot," Tom explained.

Those are some of the clean ones. Here's a twist on the old Tom Swift game, a seductive dialogue cast in less wholesome adverbial and verbal puns. The scenario begins in a bar:

"May I buy you a drink?" said Tom wryly.

"I guess so," she whined.

"We could both get stoned at my place," said Tom adamantly.

"No, let's go to my room," she said gamely.

"I'd love to come up for a visit," Tom guessed.

"Then let's go. I live in a garret apartment," she said loftily.

"Fair enough," said Tom with rising excitement.

"When we get there, we'll play around," she said skittishly.

[They arrive.]

"Now that we're here, shall I play the piano for you?" she said grandly.

"I prefer a blow job on the sax," Tom trumpeted.

"All right," she said hornily.

"Can you play in tune?" said Tom sharply.

"I guess not," she said flatly.

"Shall we go to your bedroom?" said Tom invitingly.

"My bed has good springs," she said coyly.

"I'd love to fuck you," Tom dickered.

"All right, but remember that I'm not a prostitute," she said tartly and hoarily.

"I've got to go to the bathroom first," Tom stalled.

"It's right over there," she said cannily.

"I won't be long," said Tom pithily.

"Good," she said onomatopoeically.

"I'm all done now," Tom flushed.

"Please brush your teeth," she said breathily.

"Oops, I dropped my toothpaste," said Tom, crestfallen.

[He enters the bedroom.]

"I think I'll take off my nightgown," she said silkily.

"You have a gorgeous body," said Tom figuratively.

"Want to nibble on my nipples?" she said succinctly.

"Sure. Let me remove your bra," snapped Tom.

"All right," she said, making a clean breast of things.

"Boy, you've got great boobs," said Tom titillatingly.

"Why don't you take off your trousers now?" she panted.

"I'd like to start by kissing your feet," said Tom soulfully.

"Are you sure?" she said callously.

"Absolutely," said Tom archly.

"You're making me wet," she said fluently.

"Are you all ready to go at it?" said Tom stiffly.

"First, take your dick out of that elastic band," she said jocularly.

"OK, I'm all set," said Tom cockily.

"Mmmm. That looks good," she said, feeling crotchety.

"I'm glad you like it," said Tom testily.

"Wow! Your dick is so big," she said longingly.

"You're absolutely right," said Tom straightforwardly.

"I'm all ready to go," she said receptively.

"Thanks," said Tom pointedly.

"Did you bring condoms?" she said safely.

"No I didn't," said Tom apparently.

"Well, here's one of mine. It'll help prevent VD," she said rashly.

"I don't really need one," said Tom inconceivably.

"Use one anyway," she said expectantly and pregnantly.

"Let's get to it!" probed Tom, driving home his point.

"Yes, let's!" she said, cracking up.

"Am I in deep enough?" said Tom penetratingly.

"Absolutely," she said entrancingly.

"I love your cunt," said Tom pussily.

"I love your penis," she said peckishly.

"Let's do it some more," Tom riposted.

"Fine by me," she rejoined.

"I love this stuff," Tom bawled.

"Me too!" she said movingly.

"How about you getting on top now?" said Tom flippantly.

"Sure," she said with mounting excitement.

Doggy style

"How about doing it back door?" said Tom sheepishly.

"Sure, I love to do it doggy style," she said sternly.

"OK, let's go at it," Tom lambasted.

"Fine by me," she said cheekily.

"I love doggy sex," muttered Tom.

"Me too," she said pugnaciously.

"I'll take off my boxer shorts," said Tom doggedly.

"Hurry up," she bitched.

"How about nine more times?" said Tom asininely.

"Sure," she rebutted and was taken aback.

"Oops, I just farted," said Tom astutely.

"Phew. You'd better get off me," she bridled hoarsely.

"No, I'm really getting close to orgasm," said Tom becomingly.

"So am I!" she said, whetting his appetite.

"Yyyeeeeeeeee!" Tom ejaculated.

"Ooohhhhhhhhh!" she said climactically.

"I came in like a lion!" said Tom pridefully.

"And out like a lamb," she bleated.

"And now my cock's tired," said Tom softly.

"So's my pussy," she mused

"I need a rest now," Tom derided.

"Me too," she delayed

"Screwing is so depleting," said Tom limply.

"I agree," she said dryly.

"I always feel so spent after intercourse," said Tom excruciatingly.

"Frankly, my dear, I don't give a damn," she said rhetorically.

# Classroom Classics

### The Ultimate Gift

Just before the start of Christmas vacation, the teacher asks the members of the class what gifts they hope to receive for the holidays.

"A set of electric trains," says Jimmy.

"A new CD player," says Mary.

"A box of Tampax," adds Benny.

"Tampax?" exclaims the teacher. "What on earth are you going to do with Tampax?"

"Anything I want. I keep hearing on TV how with Tampax you can go bicycling, camping, swimming, horseback riding. . . ."

### Creative Usage

During a class in grammar the teacher asks the students if anyone can illustrate the proper uses of the verbs *lie* and *lay* in a single sentence. "I know, teacher," volunteers one little boy, with waving hand.

"All right, Georgie, give us your sentence."

"The boy and the girl lie on the beach in the morning, and they lay on the beach at night."

## Under a Spell

The students at the English country school are excited that one of their own, a humble stableboy, has reached the finals of the county spelling bee. One by one the contestants drop out until only two remain, the stableboy and the daughter of a wealthy mayor.

Everyone waits eagerly for the word to be announced: "How do you spell *auspices?*"

The stableboy loses.

## Eyes on the Prize

The local Parent Teachers Association is running a lottery.

"Third prize—a thirty-two-inch color television—goes to Mrs. Carson!"

"Second prize—a cookbook—goes to Mr. Jennings!"

"Wait a minute!" grouses Joe Jennings to his wife. "How come Myrtle Carson gets a big color television as third prize and I get a lousy cookbook for second?"

"That's because the cookbook is written by the president of the PTA, and she's even signed it," explains Mrs. Jennings.

"Big deal!" whispers Joe. "Fuck the president of the PTA!"

"But that's first prize."

## A Lengthy Story

A little seventh-grader is taking a piss in the the high school boys' room when in rushes a twelfth-grader, pulls out his huge tool, and rushes to the nearest urinal.

As the seventh-grader is furtively admiring the length and thickness of the senior's equipment, the older boy says, "Whew! I just made it!" and proceeds to urinate with Niagara-like hydro-power.

"Gee, if you just made it," simpers the seventh-grader, "could you make one for me, too?"

## Casting a Spell

TEACHER: "Please spell the word *Mississippi*."
BOY: "M-I-S-S-I-S-S-I-I."
TEACHER: "Where's the P-P?"
BOY: "Running down my leg."

## Fangs a Lot

What did the vampire say to the English teacher?
"See you next period."

## How to Flunk a Sex Education Test

1. Q. What are the fallopian tubes?
   A. The subway system in Athens.

2. Q. What is a urethra?
   A. A female soul singer.

3. Q. What is an anus?
   A. Part of a famous comedy team.

4. Q. What is a testicle?
   A. An octopus's arm.

5. Q. What is a diaphragm?
   A. A figure in geometry.

6. Q. What is cunnilingus?
   A. An Irish airline.

7. Q. What is fellatio?
   A. The first name of Mr. Hornblower.

8. Q. What is a vulva?
   A. A Swedish car.

9. Q. What is a penis?
   A. Liberace.

10. Q. What is a gonad?
    A. A person who wanders from place to place.

11. Q. What is a seminal vesicle?
    A. An Everglades boat.

12. Q. What is a crotch?
    A. Something that injured people use.

13. Q. What is coitus?
    A. A throwing game played with a circle of rope.

14. Q. What is the vas deferens?
    A. A great discrepancy.

15. Q. What is sodomy?
    A. The science of growing grass.

16. Q. What are the genitals?
    A. People of non-Jewish origin.

17. Q. What is copulation?
    A. Intercourse between two consenting officers.

18. Q. What is a G-string?
    A. A part of a violin.

19. Q. What is Kotex?
    A. A radio station in Norman, Oklahoma.

20. Q. What is a cunt?
    A. A famous German philosopher.

21. Q. What are the bowels?
    A. They are A, E, I, O, and U.

22. Q. What does *congenital* mean?
    A. Friendly.

23. Q. What is D & C?
    A. Where Washington is.

24. Q. What is urine?
    A. The opposite of "you're out."

25. Q. What is a secretion?
    A. The hiding of something.

26. Q. What is a hot flash?
    A. A late-breaking news story.

27. Q. What is the menstrual cycle?
    A. A means of transportation.

28. Q. What is a vagina?
    A. A medical term for a heart attack.

29. Q. What is semen?
    A. A bunch of sailors.

30. Q. What is the anus?
    A. *Anus* is a Latin term for "yearly."

31. Q. What is a pubic hair?
    A. A wild rabbit.

32. Q. Define the term *masturbate*.
    A. What you use to catch large fish.

33. Q. What is an umbilical cord?
    A. Part of a parachute.

34. Q. What is a condom?
    A. A large apartment complex.

35. Q. What is an erection?.
    A. When Japanese people vote.

# Erotic English

English is the most widely spoken language in the history of our planet, the native or official language of forty-five countries occupying one-fifth of the earth's land surface. It is a language growing in popularity and gaining thousands of new speakers each year.

It is now time to face the fact that English is also one of the most erotically suggestive languages that has ever been procreated. Research into the origins of many English words bares all kinds of unmentionable objects, sexual body parts, and antisocial acts.

One of those acts is farting. An early meaning of *fizzle,* for example, was "to break wind without noise." *Pumpernickel* derives from the German *pumpern,* "to break wind," and *Nickel,* "devil or rascal." The idea, apparently, is that those who eat the heavy, dark, hard-to-digest rye bread are liable to be smitten by a diabolical flatulence.

When Hamlet says, " 'Tis the sport to have the engineer hoist with his own petard," he is referring to an explosive device, but *petard* goes all the way back to the Latin *peditum,* signifying the expulsion of intestinal gas. *Partridge* flies from the Greek *perdesthai,* "to break wind," so called from the whirring noise of the bird's wings when it is flushed from cover, and *feisty* scampers from the Middle English *fysten,* "break wind."

*Skulduggery* has nothing to do with grave digging, but, rather, issues from the Scottish *scukldudrie,* "fornication, adultery."

*Poppycock* may mean nonsense to you, but the word issues from the Dutch *pappekak,* "soft shit." An early Dutch word for the butterfly was *boterschijte,* suggesting that the insect acquired its name from the color of its excrement. The shitepoke heron is so called because of the way it empties its bowels when it is frightened by a shot.

Shit (in this case the German *Scheisse)* also courses through the guts of *shyster,* originally the incompetent fellow who couldn't control his bowels.

More fluidly, *addled* flows from *adel,* the Middle English word for urine; *diabetes* from a Greek word literally meaning "a passing through," referring to the tendency of those suffering from diabetes to urinate excessively; and *soluble* from Late French and Latin words that meant "not subject to constipation."

Some etymologists swear that *testimony* and *testify* are akin to the testicles. In Latin, *testiculi* meant "little witnesses" because that part of a man's body testified to the bearer's virility. Men once placed their hands on their precious gonads when swearing to tell the truth, the whole truth, and nothing but the truth. We find an allusion to this action in the biblical book of Genesis 24:2, 3, and 9: "And Abraham said unto his eldest servant of his house, that ruled over all he had, Put, I pray thee, thy hand under my thigh: And I will make thee swear by the Lord, the God of heaven, and the God of earth, that thou shalt not take a wife unto my son of the daughters of the Canaanites, among whom I dwell. . . . And the servant put his hand under the thigh of Abraham his master, and sware to him concerning the matter."

Other testy derivations include *orchid, avocado,* and *bollix.* That most elegant of flowers, the orchid, is characterized by twin bulbs that bear an uncanny resemblance to male gonads. It is for these, not for its alluring blossom (which, ironically, resembles the female genitalia), that the orchid (Greek *orkhis,* "testicle") is named. The avocado started out as *ahuacatl,* an Aztec word for "testicle." Once you realize that wild, fleshy avocados were much smaller than today's cultivated fruit, you can go out and have a ball. "To bollix up" something means to ball it up, a reference to *bollocks,* an obsolete plural for male gonads.

*Seminal* is imbued with the Latin *semen,* the figurative sense being that a seminal truth is as impregnative as human semen.

*Penis* is borrowed from the Latin word for "tail," and this small tail wags in words such as *pencil,* which first meant "a paintbrush, little tail," and *penicillin,* where the penicillium cells generated from the mold resemble small brushes.

If you find all of this etymological erotica fascinating, keep in mind that the Latin *fascinare,* "to bewitch," is an offspring of *fascinum,* once a phallic amulet used to ward off evil spirits.

Now let's move from the staff to the distaff side of our erotic English language. Ardent feminists will not be happy to learn that the name of the Grand Tetons mountain range in Wyoming literally means "Big Tits" or that the adjective *irascible* comes from the Greek *oestrus,* "in heat," and *hysterical* from *hyster,* the Greek word for "womb." The ancients believed that the womb was an unfixed organ that, moving about in a woman's stomach, made her emotionally unstable. Now you know why women get *hyster*ectomies and men get *her*nias.

Further research into the etymologies of female words reveals how many of them over time have acquired lascivious connotations.

*Wench* first meant a child of either sex. *Harlot* originally referred to male gluttons, while *courtesan,* as you might guess from its root, meant simply a female member of court. *Tart* was initially a term of endearment, like *honey, cookie,* and *sweetie pie,* as was *whore*, rooted in the Latin *carus*, "dear." That's why Martin Luther's affectionate term for his little daughter was "kleine Hure" ("little dear").

Word study and wordplay reveal all manner of juicy facts about our erotic tongue. Perhaps the most pervasive font of new metaphors in the English language is the vocabulary of the computer. Have you hackers out there noticed how slyly suggestive so many of the new computer terms are? *Bang, baud, box, to couple, to enter, floppy, to go down, hard, head, joystick, male-female connector, master-slave,* and *slot*—no wonder they call the electronic pointer a *cursor!*

Many linguists contend that the number of different words a language uses to describe an object indicates the object's cultural importance. Thus, while the English language has only a single word for "walrus" and a relative few for "grass," the Eskimos have six different words to distinguish among the varieties of walrus and the Hawaiians a vast array of words to describe each kind of grass. Some observers have drawn significance from the fact that Arabic has more than three hundred words for sword while the Eskimo language has none for war.

What, then, can we conclude about the values of English speakers in light of a survey published in *Playboy* magazine that lists no fewer than three hundred different names, epithets, and euphemisms in English for female breasts? *Bazooms, boobs, bubbles, hooters, jugs, knockers, lungs, mammaries, maracas, melons, a pair,* and *tits* are but a dozen among the titillating terms.

An anagram is the rearrangement of all the letters in a word or phrase to make a new word or phrase. For example, a slight rearrangement of the letters in *bedroom* yields *boredom*. Here are some more erotic anagrams:

| | |
|---|---|
| masturbate | rubs at meat |
| sexual intercourse | our lust an exercise |
| striptease | peer tit, ass |

Is it just coincidence that there are five parts of the body that can be anagrammed into four other body parts and all four rearrangements involve corporeal equipment that is not to be mentioned in polite company?

*Spine* yields *penis*.

*Elbow* yields *bowel*.

*Torso* yields *roots*.

*Ears* yields *arse*.

The most arcane transformation involves the word *suture*, defined not only as the stitching of a wound or opening, but also as the juncture of two bones, especially of the skull. If we accept *suture* as a kind of body part, we come up with the anagrammatical *uterus*.

In 1988 James H. Price and Edwin B. Steen came out with a book titled *Human Sex and Sexuality* (Dover). Shake up the letters in the last names of the authors—*Pricesteen*—and *erect penis* sticks out!

An acronym is a word formed from the initial letters of other words. ZIP codes, from "Zone Improvement Plan," reputedly add *zip* to our mail. Truth In Testing laws have required the College Board to make available previously administered SAT examinations. Have you noted the full implications of the acronym formed by "Truth In Testing"?

A palindrome (from Greek word parts that mean "to run backward") is a special kind of anagram in which a word or phrase is spelled exactly the same forward and backward. Many a woman would be surprised to learn that she has palindromic breasts—a *tit*, a *boob*, and a *pap*.

Erections might be palindromically defined as *stiff fits*, the smell of love as *amor aroma*, and fellatio as *gnaw wang*. One of the best and truest of palindromic statements is *sex at noon taxes*. Other erotic palindromes include *A slut nixes sex in Tulsa*, Tulsa nightlife: *Filth, gin, a slut, Traci tore erotic art, Sex-aware era waxes,* and *Egad! No bondage!*

A semordnilap (*palindromes* in reverse) is the spelling of a word from back to front to make another word, as in *diaper-repaid*. Those who play golf attach ironic significance to the fact that *golf* spelled backward is *flog*. What, then, are we to make of the fact that *eros* spelled backward is *sore*?

Back in 1953, the Rabelaisian Welsh poet Dylan Thomas wrote a lyrically dramatic work about life and love and death in a small Welsh town. He entitled his poetic statement *Llareggub,* and everyone found the title to be charmingly and liltingly Welsh in sound—everyone, that is, until Thomas, deep in his cups at a party one night, drunkenly confessed that Llareggub was simply a reversal of the words *bugger all.*

Thomas's publishers quickly changed the title to *Under Milk Wood.*

Start reading the names of commercial products semordnila-pally, and you'll discover surprising messages. Evian mineral water, for example, comes out as *naive,* which makes you wonder if they're putting something over on us. Now take a backward glance at Dial (soap), Tums (stomach pills), and Tulsa (gasoline). Voilà!—*laid, smut,* and *a slut.*

No wonder that the poet T. Eliot often wrote pessimistic poems. What would you do if your name were *toilet* spelled backward? Staying with famous names, humorist Dave Barry has pointed out that the name *Spiro Agnew* is an anagram of *grow a penis.* And actress Alice Faye, who was married to Phil Harris, has a name that is Pig Latin for *phallus.*

Have you ever noticed how many place-names are richly filthy? Clustered near Lancaster, Pennsylvania, we have the Pennsylvania Dutch towns of Intercourse, Blueball, and Bird In Hand. In Long Island sits the city of Flushing, in Thailand the masturbatory Bangkok, and in Newfoundland Come-By-Chance, Dildo, Blow-Me-Down, and Bunghole Tickle.

But the British Isles are the richest repository of salacious,

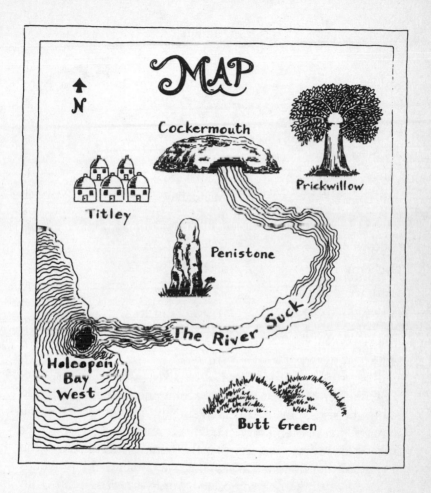

The British Isles are the richest repository of salacious,
suggestive place-names.

suggestive place-names. Each of the following is authentic, certified, and genuine; none is made up:

| | |
|---|---|
| Acocks Green | Horden |
| Aspull | Laide |
| Assloss | Laytown |
| Bitch Burn | Little Cocklick |
| Breaston | Little Coxwell |
| Broadbottom | Long Load |
| Bungay | Maidenhead |
| Butt Green | Mandallay |
| Buttock's Booth | Penistone |
| Chicklade | Peterhead |
| Cockermouth | Pishill |
| Cummeenduff Glen | Prickwillow |
| Diddlebury | The Pole of Itlow |
| Freeby | The River Suck |
| Holeopen Bay West | Titley |

A number of feminists have become increasingly concerned about the sexism of third person singular pronouns in English. While *I, you, we,* and *they* contain no references to gender, *he* and *she* do. Some who feel that the issue is full of sound and fury signifying nothing suggest that we combine the pronouns *he* or *she* or *it* into one compacted word—*h'orsh'it.*

Many words can be cut up or divided into parts that are themselves complete words. *Inflation,* for example, can be made to yield up *in* + *flat* + *ion* (or *I* + *on*). Such divisions are called charades.

If a boy and a girl are *amiable together,* the boy may begin to wonder, *"Am I able to get her?"*

And just a thought for all you women out there: MENtal illness, MENstrual cramps, MENopause. Ever notice how all of women's problems start with men? And when you have real problems, it's HISterectomy. And don't forget the GUYnecologist.

Why is it, we may wonder, that *therapist* is *the rapist* in disguise?

An oxymoron is not a big dumb cow, but rather a figure of speech in which two incongruous, contradictory terms are yoked together in a small space, as in *old news* and *original copy*. My favorite oxymoron is *flat busted*.

How come in England you can say things like "I'll come by in the morning and knock you up," "Be sure that your pencil has a rubber on it," and "I'll give you a blow as soon as I get the news" and not get slapped in the face?

Other Briticisms demonstrate the truth of George Bernard Shaw's dictum that "England and America are two countries separated by a common language": The archbishop of Canterbury once consoled the cathedral's professional tenor, who had complained that if his overdue paycheck did not come soon, he would have to cancel his plans to get married. "There, there. Keep your pecker up," said the archbishop, "and the screw will come!" In translation, all the holy man said was "Keep your spirit up, and the money will come!"

Or, as the great line from Gilbert and Sullivan's *Trial by Jury* goes, "Be firm be firm, my pecker! Your evil star's ascendant!"

# Hysterical History

'Tis said that Cleopatra bathed in ass's milk. No wonder she made such an asp of herself. When she put the asp to her breast, she sang, "Fangs for the Mammaries."

Over the centuries, a number of time honored dirty anecdotes have become identified with the Queen of Denial and with other historical personages. Some of these salacious stories may be true, some may not. Who cares? They're fun, and they lighten and enlighten our oral history.

## A Horsa of a Different Color

Hengist and Horsa were two Norse brothers who, according to tradition, led the Jute invasion of Britain. Hengist raised sheep, and Horsa raised donkeys. It wasn't long before Britain was overrun by Hengist's sheep and Horsa's asses.

## A Penetrating Definition

The French actor and dramatist Molière once wrote that "Writing is like prostitution. First you do it for the love of it. Then you do it for your friends. And finally you end up doing it for money."

## Same Difference

The English playwright Richard Brinsley Sheridan was once attacked by an eighteenth-century feminist who demanded an answer to her question, "Is there any real difference between a man and a woman?"

"The difference?" replied Sheridan. "That I cannot conceive."

## Revolutionary Thoughts

In a little-known essay, Benjamin Franklin suggested adding certain chemicals to food so that those ingesting them would break wind aromatically, rather than malodorously. The title of Franklin's essay is "Fart Proudly." If you think I'm kidding, look for the essay in a nearby library.

Supporting the American Revolution, Franklin declared, "We must all hang together, or assuredly we shall all hang separately." He persuaded so many of his countrymen to revolt against the rule of the British that America became the most well-hung nation in history.

The great American hero of the Revolutionary War was, of course, George Washington. When Washington was a little boy, he chopped down a tree for a cherry. When he got a little older, he learned to get cherries by spreading limbs.

## Define Your Terms

The great American dictionary maker Noah Webster was a renowned philanderer. One day Mrs. Webster found the wordsman in bed with the chambermaid.

"Noah, I am surprised," huffed the offended wife.

Thereupon Webster drew himself up righteously and informed her, "No, madam, you are astonished. I am surprised."

## Honest Abe

Abraham Lincoln attended a church bazaar and, in payment for a sprig of violets, tendered a $20 bill to the woman behind the booth. She made no effort to offer change and gushed, "Oh, thank you, Mr. President!"

Lincoln reached down from his great height and gently patted the woman's breasts. "What are these, my dear?" he asked.

"Why, Mr. Lincoln, they're my breasts. What did you think they were?"

"Well," said the president. "Everything else is so high around here, I wanted to be sure they weren't your buttocks."

## Plaque Fact

No one knows how many wives Mormon leader Brigham Young had, but the simple marker at his birthplace in Whitingham, Vermont, offers a clue: "Brigham Young, born on this spot, 1801, a man of much courage and superb equipment."

## A Bright Idea

The great inventor Thomas Edison once visited a Sioux settlement where he found an outhouse that had no heat or light. Touched by the plight of those who had to sit there in the dark and cold, the Wizard of Menlo Park installed electricity in the outhouse. Ever since, Edison has been known as the first man ever to wire a head for a reservation.

## The Price Is Right

George Bernard Shaw once asked a noblewoman if she would have sex with him for a million pounds.

"Why, yes, I think I would," she replied.

"How about for a hundred thousand pounds?" he continued.

"Well, for a hundred thousand, I guess I would."

Shaw then asked her, "Would you have sex with me for two pounds?"

She was shocked. "For two measly pounds! What do you think I am?"

"We've settled that," Shaw told her. "Now we're just haggling about the price."

## Prudery and Rudery

Winston Churchill dined at the home of a social luminary who possessed strongly Victorian views about appropriate language. For the main course chicken à l'orange was served and Churchill asked for "a breast."

"Sir Winston," the hostess huffed, "we don't talk about breasts of chicken here. We talk about white meat." Churchill apologized profusely.

The next day the woman received a small corsage from her guest of honor. The accompanying card read: "Dear Madam: In recognition of our lovely time together last evening, I hope that you will wear these flowers on your white meat."

## Short and Sweet

*New Yorker* writer Dorothy Parker went away on her honeymoon. After several weeks she received a letter from her editor, Harold Ross, asking her to send in an overdue story she was supposed to have written.

Parker sent back a telegram that read, "Too fucking busy—and vice versa."

Parker wrote a report about a Yale prom in which the number and beauty of the girls present had apparently made a deep impression on her: "If all those sweet young things were laid end to end—I wouldn't be at all surprised."

When asked to use the word *horticulture* in a sentence, Parker replied: "You can lead a horticulture, but you can't make her think."

## And How Was Runch?

Prior to World War II, Franklin Roosevelt was holding high-level talks with officials of the Japanese government. During a formal breakfast, Eleanor Roosevelt asked a Japanese diplomat sitting next to her if he had had a good election the day before.

The fellow turned crimson and attempted to change the subject by saying, "Yes, and are you enjoying your bleakfast?"

## Once More with Feeling

The platinum-blond movie actress Jean Harlow is said to have said, "I like to wake up each morning feeling a new man," to which Groucho Marx has added, "You're only as old as the woman you feel."

Harlow was introduced to Lady Margot Asquith, wife of British prime minister Herbert Henry Asquith. Harlow insisted on addressing the lady by her first name and made the further mistake of pronouncing the name as if it rhymed with *cot*. Lady Asquith corrected her, "My dear, the *t* is silent, as in *Harlow*."

## Life, Liberty, and the Pursuit

General Charles de Gaulle and his wife were attending a dinner party at the American embassy. After a sumptuous meal, the American ambassador asked each guest to name what he or she wanted most from life.

"Peace," answered one member of the party; "excitement," answered another.

When Mrs. de Gaulle gave her response, everyone on the American staff blushed crimson—until the great man explained to his wife, "My dear, you should pronounce that *happiness,* not *a penis.*"

## Cut the Crap

Being from Missouri, Harry S. Truman often talked to farm groups. Whenever he held forth about fertilizer, he always used the word *manure,* much to the embarrassment of his support staff.

When the public relations people went to Mrs. Truman to ask her help in getting the president to stop using the offending word, she sighed, "You'd be amazed how long it took me to get Harry to start using *manure.*"

## Starstruck

A famous actress persisted in bothering film director Alfred Hitchcock about his camera angles. Day after day the actress nagged the great filmmaker to photograph her from her "best side."

Finally, Hitchcock's patience was exhausted. "My dear," he explained, "we can't photograph your best side because you're always sitting on it!"

## A Thorny Problem

Soon after he came to the Senate in 1949, Lyndon B. Johnson tried for the minority leadership position in the Democratic caucus. He thought he had the position locked up, but when he emerged from the Senate caucus chamber, he had only a handful of votes.

Asked by reporters to explain his overwhelming defeat, Johnson replied, "As a senator from Texas, I have just learned the difference between a cactus and a caucus. In a cactus all the pricks are on the outside."

## Sign of the Times

In 1973, President Richard M. Nixon appointed Harvard Law School professor Archibald Cox as U.S. Special Prosecutor for the Watergate hearings. When Cox began to reveal the Watergate break-in and cover-up, the president decided that his appointee was pursuing his charge too zealously. So he fired him.

Very soon the most popular bumper sticker in America became "Nixon is a Cox Sacker."

## Fore Play

The world's worst golfing foursome—Monica Lewinsky, O. J. Simpson, Ted Kennedy, and Bill Clinton.

Why? you ask.

Well, Monica Lewinsky is a hooker.

O. J. Simpson is a slicer.

Ted Kennedy can't drive over the water.

And Bill Clinton can't remember the last hole he played.

## Bush + Gore = Gush + Bore

The presidential battle between George Bush and Al Gore was one of the most hotly contested in history. But the two candidates did agree that Hollywood films are too explicit. Bush complained that movies are too violent and Gore that they are too sexual.

In other words, Bush felt that there's too much gore, and Gore felt that there's too much bush.

# Titillating Titles

It is a little-known fact that the titles of novels, stories, and poems are heavily censored by the publishing industry. Many a writer has been frustrated by having his or her titles castrated—altered from something unique to something eunuch. Even William Shakespeare had to change the titles of his plays from *The King's John, A Midsummer Night's Cream, Ass—You Lick It, Antony and Clitopatra, King Leer, Coriol Anus, Julius Seize Her, Tight-Ass Androgynous, Coitus and Cressida,* and *Romeo and Julie Et Each Other* to placate his nervous editors.

Through exhaustive research, I have been able to uncover the original, uncut, unfixed titles of many classics. In the interest of literary scholarship and writerly integrity, I share my findings with you:

- *The Adventures of Fuckleberry Finn*
- *Animal Firm*

- *Anthony Perverse*
- *Arouse for Emily*
- *Arse Poetica*
- *The Ass Burn Papers*
- *Asshole on Ice*
- *The Autobiography of Malcolm's Sex*
- *The Autoerotic of the Breakfast Table*
- *A Backward Glans o'er Traveled Roads*
- *The Balled Soprano*
- *The Bare*
- *Bend Her*
- *Brazen in the Sun*
- *Bride's Head Revisited*
- *The Buggery American*
- *Buns and Shovers*
- *The Celibate Jumping Frog of Calavaras County*
- *The Cocks Go In and Dent*
- *Come Blow Your Porn*
- *A Confederacy of Douches*
- *The Confessions of Nat Turn Her*
- *The Cunterbury Tails*
- *Dames People Lay*
- *The Deerlayer*
- *The Diamond as Big as the Tits*
- *An Enema of the People*
- *The Erections*
- *For Whom the Balls Toil*

- *From Here to Maternity*
- *Fucky Quim*
- *Gentlemen Prefer Glands*
- *The Gold Buggery*
- *The Goniad*  ,
- *Great Expectorations*
- *The Harlot Letter*
- *Heart of Dorkness*
- *Heaves of Ass*
- *Intimations of Immorality*
- *Jude the Obscene*
- *Kubla's Can*
- *Lay Miserably*
- *Look to the Mountin'*
- *Lost Whore Risin'*
- *The Love-Schlong of J. Alfred Prudefuck*
- *The Lust Weak End*
- *Madame Ovary*
- *Mammaries of Things Past*
- *The Man Who Came at Dinner*
- *The Man Without a Cunt*
- *Moby's Dick*
- *The Mooning and Sex Pants*
- *Mother Goosed Rhymes*
- *The Myth of Syphilis*
- *The Naked in the Bed*
- *Oldest Living Confederate Widow Smells All*

- *One Flew Over the Cuckold's Nest*
- *The Organ of the Feces*
- *The Outcasts of Poke Her Flat*
- *Pecker's Bad Boy*
- *Phallus in Wonderland*
- *The Pick Prick Papers*
- *Pilgrim's Congress*
- *Portrait of the Fartist as a Young Man*
- *The Prying of Lot 49*
- *The Rectum of Just In*
- *Remembrance of Things Pederast*
- *The Rise of Silas's Lap Ham*
- *Root*
- *The Round and the Furry*
- *The Scarlet Pimp*
- *She Shtups to Conquer*
- *Shithartha*
- *The Short Crappy Life of Francis Macomber*
- *Sister Hairy*
- *The Slime of Miss Jean's Body*
- *The Snatcher in the Rye*
- *Snatch-22*
- *Some Came, Running*
- *The Son Also Rises*
- *The Spy Who Shoved Me*
- *Tails from Uncle Ream Us*
- *The Tell-Tale Fart*

*One Flew Over the Cuckold's Nest*

- *Uncle Tom's Grabbin'*
- *The Valley of Whores*
- *Whore and Piece*
- *Your Assic Park*

# Beyond Wordplay

Back in the introduction (you do read introductions, don't you?) I said that these pages would feature dirty wordplay exclusively. Well, I lied a little.

You see, there actually are some raunchy jokes that are not built on verbal diddling but that still manage to be humorous. I figure that now that I have your attention, I can't resist seizing by the you-know-whats the opportunity to lay on you some choice examples of nonverbal smut. So by popular self-request I close this book with my dozen all-time favorite, unpunny, but nonetheless funny, lewd stories.

## A Truncated Story

Three white hunters are out stalking game in the African bush when each meets with a terrible accident:

A charging lion gouges out the eye of the first hunter. A monkey in a tree hurls a coconut that destroys the inner ear of the second. And an onrushing elephant steps on and crushes the penis of the third.

The three men are carried near unto death into the closest village, where the witch doctor, hoping to save their lives, instructs the villagers to go out and kill the offending beasts and bring back their carcasses.

After the deed is done, the witch doctor scoops out the eye of the dead lion and, with the aid of herbs and incantations, places that eye into the hollow socket of the first hunter. In the second hunter's aural passage he inserts the inner ear of the monkey. Then the doctor hacks off the elephant's trunk and grafts it onto the third hunter's crotch.

A year later the three hunters arrange a reunion at the Harvard Club of New York, and, as you might predict, they soon start talking about their lives since their accidents in Africa.

"Life has been terrific!" exults the first hunter. "I quickly learned that lions have fantastic vision, and with this lion's eye I can see incredible distances, even beyond horizons. For the first time in my life I can really appreciate paintings and films and the colors of sunrises and sunsets."

Now it's the second hunter's turn: "My life has been very beautiful, too. With this monkey's ear I can hear whispers in distant rooms and birds in distant trees. I've never appreciated before how beautiful are the sounds of nature, and of the city, for all that matter. And the experience of music is nearly orgasmic for me."

The two of them turn to the third hunter and inquire, "Well, how's it been for you, George?"

"Things have been great for me, too," George grins. "My sex life has been extraordinary. Ever since Africa I've been in seventh heaven and on cloud nine—and so have the ladies. They just love this thing between my legs. It's so long, so thick, so sensitive, so manipulable. But, guys, to tell the truth, I do have one annoying problem. It's so damned embarrassing at cocktail parties when people start passing the peanuts."

## Having a Blastoff

Joe is chosen to be the astronaut riding on the first manned rocket to Mars. The big day arrives, and Joe dons his space suit, screws on his bubble helmet, enters the ship, and straps himself in. "10-9-8," the countdown begins. "7-6-5—oops, a thick cloud cover has descended on the base, and liftoff is postponed."

So the next day, they try again. Joe puts on his suit and helmet, enters the craft, and straps himself in—and again a mysterious cloud cover enshrouds the area and again the launch is put off.

This happens ten days in a row, and Joe's nerves are completely ajangle. So he goes to his tall, shapely girlfriend Nancy and says, "Honey, I've got to have a day off or I'll have a nervous breakdown. I want you to take my place tonight. As usual, the cloud cover will come in to postpone the liftoff, and I'll take over the next day."

Congenial Nancy agrees, and the next day she slips into the gear, enters the ship, and awaits another aborted countdown. "10-9-8"—no cloud cover—"7-6-5"—no cloud cover—"4-3-2-1 BLASTOFF!!!" The rocket lifts off, the force of gravity increases, and Nancy, who has had no training in how to nullify the effects of extra Gs, blacks out.

Mission control immediately switches the ship to autoland, and Nancy wakes up in the base's hospital emergency room. Medical personnel are swirling around her while a doctor is squatting atop her hips and pushing down with great force on her breasts.

"Where am I, and what the hell is going on here?" Nancy gasps.

"Stay calm, Joe," puffs the doctor. "We're just trying to force your testicles back down. We think if we do, your cock'll pop back out!"

## A Whale of a Sperm

Charlie the Sperm is an unusually ambitious little fellow. He's really working out, swimming lap after lap, lifting weight after weight, and doing push-up after push-up, sit-up after sit-up, and chin-up after chin-up. The other sperm ask, "Charlie, what's with all this exercise stuff? Why don't you just relax and enjoy life, like the rest of us?"

"Look, guys," says Charlie, "out there, at the end of the tunnel, there's a big round thing, and it's called an egg. One day an alarm's going to go off, and only one among the millions of us gets to unite with that egg. That lucky sperm, the fastest and strongest among us, will get to be part of a new life, and I want to be the one!"

Charlie continues to work out like crazy, and, sure enough, one day things really begin to heat up and the alarm does sound. The sperm all start wriggling madly upstream, but Charlie bursts from the starting line, leaps into the semen, cuts through the goo with powerful undulations, and pulls way out ahead of all the others. As Charlie begins to disappear over the semen falls, the other sperm sigh, "Well, good old Charlie has worked hard for this moment. He certainly deserves the first shot at the egg."

Then they see Charlie frantically swimming against the tide back towards them and waving and yelling something. They strain to hear and finally pick up what he's shouting: "Go back, everybody! Go back! It's a blow job!"

## You Can't Beat This Tattoo

A man staggers into a doctor's office. He's deathly pale, all out of breath, and perspiring profusely. The doctor helps him remove his clothes and gives him a quick examination. "Sir," the doctor diagnoses, "you are suffering from a massive respiratory breakdown. If your system doesn't receive vigorous stimulation within ten minutes, you are in grave danger of dying. Now fortunately, I've got three nurses in the back room who stand ready to give you a collective massage, and that should get you through this crisis."

"Sure, Doc, anything you say," gasps the man, and he passes out.

The doctor wheels the patient into the back room, and the three nurses start kneading his pale body. As they're administering the treatment, they notice that he's got the smallest pecker they've ever seen, and on that pecker is a tattoo that says TINY.

The three nurses start giggling and then riotously laughing, and this makes their massaging even more vigorous. Pretty soon the man's breathing becomes regular, his color returns, and he leaves the office the picture of perfect health.

The next day the telephone rings, and one of the nurses picks it up and starts guffawing. "Hey, girls, remember that guy with the little pecker with TINY tattooed on it? He's so grateful that we saved his life that he wants to take us all out for dinner. Now I don't know about you, but I'm not going out with some guy with a little pecker with TINY tattooed on it."

The second nurse agrees, but the third one says, "Look, Mabel, I'm a little hard up for money these days, and I can use a good meal. Tell the guy that he can pick me up here after work tonight."

The next day the third nurse shows up at the office. She's got a very satisfied smile on her face, and she's absolutely glowing. In fact, she's looking positively transformed, transfigured, transmuted, and transfixed.

"Doris," inquire the other nurses, "you're looking incredibly happy. What happened last night with that patient and you?"

"After a delicious dinner," she tosses back her head and laughs, "we went back to his apartment, hopped into the sack, and had the most incredible sex I've ever experienced!"

"How could that happen with a guy who's got such a little pecker with TINY tattooed on it?"

"Because," smirks the nurse, "when that little pecker got big, you could read the whole message: TINY'S KOSHER DELICA-

TESSEN AND CATERERS. LOCATED ON THE CORNER OF MAIN STREET AND SPRUCE AVENUE. WE BAKE ON THE PREMISES AND DELIVER WITHIN A HALF HOUR. CALL 345-6789."

## Gorilla Warfare

A man visits the zoo and goes to the monkey house to look at his favorite exhibit—a huge, hairy gorilla.

This particular day, the visitor decides to test the intelligence of the great ape, so he raises his arms, grabs the hair on his head, begins making simian noises, and waits to see how the gorilla will respond. To the man's surprise and delight, the gorilla perfectly imitates his action and sounds.

Continuing his experiment, the man starts beating his chest with his fists, all the time emitting more grunts, and the ape immediately repeats the procedure.

So the man decides to challenge the ape even further with something that is not simian. He moves in closer to the cage, sticks out his index finger, hooks it onto the lower lid of his right eye, and pulls it down.

Immediately the gorilla roars, rushes forward, grabs the man by an ear, and slaps him around hard. The stunned and battered visitor staggers to the keeper's shed and screams, "That gorilla of yours just beat the crap out of me! You've got a killer ape here! You should have it destroyed!"

"Nonsense," answers the keeper. "It's a perfectly gentle animal that's never harmed anyone before. You must have done something to anger it."

After the man denies the charge and demonstrates to the keeper exactly what he did at the cage, the keeper exclaims, "Well, no wonder you got smacked around! Don't you know that pulling down the lower lid of the eye means 'Fuck you!' in gorilla language?"

"That's absurd," whines the man. "Animals can't communicate like that," and he drags himself home from the zoo.

It takes two weeks for the man's contusions to heal, and all the time he's plotting his revenge on the ape. Once again he shows up at the gorilla's cage, and now he's carrying a shopping bag. The man and the gorilla look at each other, and again the man grabs his hair and begins an apelike grunting.

The ape grabs his hair and joins the grunting.

Then the man starts beating his chest and making more simian noises.

So does the gorilla.

Finally, the man opens the shopping bag, takes out a long, sharp knife, and tosses it into the gorilla cage.

The ape lumbers over and picks up the knife.

The man takes out a large piece of salami, sticks it between his legs, takes out another knife, whacks off a chunk of the meat, and waits to see what the gorilla will do.

The gorilla looks at the guy and pulls down his lower eyelid.

## *The High Cost of Inflation*

Neglecting to call ahead for a reservation, Harry and Bernie go to a whorehouse to disport themselves carnally. It's Saturday night, and all the prostitutes are taken up with patrons. The madam doesn't want to lose Harry's and Bernie's patronage, so she places a life-size inflatable rubber doll in their beds, figuring that the rooms will be dark and the dim-witted men will never know the difference.

The unknowing Harry and Bernie thrash around with their respective inflatable dolls, and, as they drive home, they compare experiences. "My broad was just wonderful," Harry leers. "So soft, so cooperative. But the strange thing is that the whole time we were going at it, she never said a word."

"You think yours was strange," says Bernie. "I was having a great time and we were getting it on so passionately. Then I bit her once on the tit, and she blew a big fart and flew out the window!"

## In Onion There Is Strength

A man enters the hospital for a vasectomy and says to his doctor, "Doc, I know it seems like I'm a chicken, but I'm so queasy about your performing surgery on my gonads that I want more than a local anesthetic. I want you to give me a general anesthetic to knock me out entirely." The doctor agrees and goes into the operating room with an anesthetist, who quickly puts the patient to sleep under the gas.

The doctor is having a bad day, and as he's snipping away, one of the patient's testicles shoots out of his scrotum. It bounces and then rolls across the floor, and before the doctor and his assistant can catch up, it disappears into an exposed drain hole.

"You're in deep doo-doo, Doc," says the anesthetist. "When this guy wakes up and finds one of his balls missing, he's going to slap you with one hell of a malpractice suit!"

"Not if I can find some kind of testicular replacement," says the doctor. "Give him another whiff and keep him asleep for another fifteen minutes. I'll be right back." The doctor hurries down to the hospital parking lot, and out of his car he takes a big shopping bag from a trip he has made to the supermarket just before coming to the hospital. He reaches into a plastic sack of produce and pulls out a little pearl onion. He takes the onion into the operating room and hastily sews it into the scrotum of the unconscious patient, who soon wakes up none the wiser.

Six months later the patient comes in for a checkup, and the doctor asks how things have been since the operation. "Not bad," explains the patient, "but I have had three rather strange problems."

"Oh, what could they be?" asks the doctor, rolling his eyes and nervously recalling the insertion of the pearl onion.

"Well, whenever I take a piss, I get heartburn. And whenever I make love to my wife, her eyes water. But the oddest thing of all, Doc, is that whenever I go into a McDonald's, I get an erection!"

## Don't Forget to Wear Your Rubbers

A man and a woman, each married to someone else, are making torrid love in her bedroom when they hear a key being inserted into the lock for the living room door. "Roland," gasps the unfaithful wife, "that's got to be my husband coming back a day early. Quick! Jump out of this window!"

Fortunately, they're in a ranch-style house, and Roland, completely naked except for the condom on his still-erect tool, climbs through the window onto the lawn, crawls a few yards, and hides behind a bush. Unfortunately, it's raining like crazy and he's wet and miserable, so he looks for his first opportunity to escape.

Along comes a pack of joggers, and Roland, seeing his chance, falls in step with them.

One of the men trotting next to Roland asks him, "Say, mister, do you always go running in the buff?"

"Yep."

"And do you always do your jogging wearing a condom?"

"Only when it rains."

## Venomous Humor

Two good friends are out on a camping trip, and one of them has to take a leak. He goes out to the woods to do his duty when a rattlesnake slithers out of a bush and bites him on the tip of his cock.

"Don't worry," says the other man, "I'll drive to a pay phone and call a doctor."

So the friend drives off, finds a pay phone, dials a doctor, and asks what he should do. "Well," says the doctor, "you have to cut crosses in the wound and suck out the poison."

"Is that the only way to save my friend, doctor?" asks the man.

"Yes, you must do that or he will die."

The caller drives back to camp, and his friend asks, "So, what did the doctor say?"

"He says you're gonna die."

## *Weight and See*

A four-hundred-pound man is oozing down the street when he sees a sign on a door that reads: "Amazing New Weight-Loss Plan/Come In and Try Our Amazing New Methods/First Session Free!"

Figuring that he's got nothing to lose but some adipose tissue, the man opens the door, climbs a flight of stairs, and comes to a long corridor. Along the corridor are five doors marked "Ten Pounds," "Twenty Pounds," "Thirty Pounds," "Forty Pounds," "Fifty Pounds," and "One Hundred Pounds."

The manager of the program instructs the man to take off all his clothes and to go to the Ten Pound Room. On entering, the man finds the room to be hot like a sauna, but inside there's an attractive, naked woman in sneakers. And hanging from her neck is a sign that says, "If you catch me, you can screw me."

The man lunges around the room trying to catch the woman, but he's so obese and she's so swift and agile that he fails. As he's leaving the building, the manager asks him to step on a scale, and, sure enough, he's lost ten pounds.

Naturally, the man signs up for the program, and he progresses through the Twenty, Thirty, Forty, and Fifty Pound Rooms. Each overheated room is bigger than the last, and the woman in each room is increasingly attractive, swift, and agile, so that, even with his increasing weight loss and the "If you catch me, you can screw me" signs urging him on, he can never catch any of them.

After working out in the Fifty Pound Room, the man is down to 250 pounds, and he's raring to complete his weight loss by going to the Hundred Pound Room, even though it's very expensive. The manager cheerfully takes his money, and the man walks down the corridor and opens an enormous metal door to enter the Hundred Pound Room. The door locks behind him, and the man looks up to see a huge gorilla. Around the gorilla's neck is a sign that says, "If I catch you, I'll screw you!"

## A Beastly Experience

We all remember the first time we did it, and you know what "it" means. My first time occurred when I was nineteen years old and came on to a much more experienced woman a few years older. We hit it off, one thing led to another, and we ended up in her bedroom, which was ringed with a whole menagerie of stuffed animals. We're talking about dozens and dozens of these stuffed toys, which apparently she had a fetish for collecting.

On the top shelf, she displayed the biggest dolls, somewhere around three feet high—giraffes, elephants, whales, and hippos— all the largest beasts.

On the second shelf sat lions and tigers and bears—oh my!— all around two feet high.

Next came smaller doggies and kitty cats and ponies, and on the bottom shelf reposed the smallest specimens, each about six inches high—squirrels and chipmunks and mice and bunny rabbits.

Well, somehow all this animal life stoked my libido, and we really went at it. When we were done, I rolled over, looked at my lover shyly, and confessed, "You know, that was my first time making love. I was wondering if you could tell me how I did."

She thought a bit and said, "Not bad, you can take any animal from the bottom shelf."

## The Twelve Days of Christmas

*December 14, 2003*
*Dear Roger,*

*I went to the door today and the postman delivered a partridge in a pear tree. What a thoroughly delightful gift. I couldn't have been more surprised. You're an angel.*

> *With all my love and devotion,*
> *Agnes*

The Twelve Days of Christmas

*December 15, 2003*
*Dearest Roger,*

Today the postman brought your very sweet gift. Just imagine, two turtledoves. I'm delighted at your very thoughtful gift. They are adorable and I love you for them.

> All my love,
> Agnes

*December 16, 2003*
*Dear Roger,*

Oh! Aren't you the extravagant one! Now I really must protest. I don't deserve such generosity as three French hens. They are just darling, but I must insist that you've been too kind.

> Love,
> Agnes

*December 17, 2003*
*Dear Roger,*

Today the postman delivered four calling birds. They are just beautiful, but don't you think enough is enough? You're being too romantic.

> Affectionately,
> Agnes

*December 18, 2003*
*Dearest Roger,*

What a surprise! The postman just delivered five golden rings, one for each finger. You're just impossible. Frankly, all those birds squawking were beginning to get on my nerves.

> All my love,
> Agnes

*December 19, 2003*
*Dear Roger,*

I couldn't believe my eyes this morning as I walked out onto the front porch and there were six geese a-laying on the steps. So you're back to the birds again, huh? These geese are huge. Where will I ever keep them? The neighbors are complaining and I can't sleep through the racket. I appreciate your thoughtfulness, but . . .

Please stop.

Cordially,
Agnes

### December 20, 2003
Roger,

What's with you and these fucking birds? Today I received seven swans a-swimming. What kind of a goddam joke is this? There's bird shit all over the house, and they never stop their goddam racket. I can't sleep at night, and I'm a nervous wreck.

Just knock it off with these dumbass birds, OK???

Sincerely,
Agnes

### December 21, 2003
OK Buster,

I think I prefer the birds. What the hell am I going to do with eight maids a-milking? It's not enough with all those birds and the eight milking maids, but they had to bring along their goddam cows! There's shit all over the lawn, and I can't even move in my own house.

Just lay off me, smartass!
Agnes

### December 22, 2003
Hey, Shithead,

What are you? Some kind of a sadist? Now I've got nine pipers playing, and Christ, do they play! They haven't stopped chasing those eight maids a-milking since they arrived this morning. The cows are getting upset, and they're stepping all over the screeching fucking

birds. What the hell am I supposed to do? The neighbors have started
a petition to have me evicted.

**You'll get yours, bastard,**
**Agnes**

### December 23, 2003
**You Rotten Prick,**

Who in the hell needs ten ladies dancing? I can't imagine why I
call those sluts ladies. They've been balling the pipers all night long.
The stupid cows and birds can't sleep, and the goddam racket around
here has given them diarrhea. My living room is a river of shit! The
Commissioner of Buildings has subpoenaed me to give cause why the
building should not be condemned.

I'm siccing the police on you, asshole!

**One Who Means It**

### December 24, 2003
**Listen, Peckerhead,**

What's with the eleven lords a-leaping—on all those maids and
ladies? Some of those poor broads will never walk again. The pipers
have run through the maids and gang-banged the ladies, and they're
now committing sodomy on the cows. The twenty-three birds were
trampled in the orgy and are now all dead. I hope you're satisfied,
you rotten, vicious bastard!

**I hate your guts, dumbshit,**
**Agnes**

### December 26, 2003
**Dear Sir:**

This is to acknowledge your latest gift of twelve fiddlers fiddling,
which you have seen fit to inflict on our client, Ms. Agnes Mendelstone. As you no doubt have guessed, the destruction of her property
was total. Be advised that all future correspondence with our client
should be cleared through this law office, Badger and Bender.

*I feel compelled to warn you that if you should attempt to reach Ms. Mendelstone at Happy Dale Sanitarium, the attendants of that institution have instructions to shoot you on sight. With this letter please find attached a warrant for your arrest.*

**Season's Greetings,**
**Frank Bender**